Unit D

Mountains and Molehills

Rocks, Minerals, and Landforms

I WONDER

Science begins with wondering. What do you wonder about when you see land like that shown?

Work with a partner to make a list of questions you may have about land. Be ready to share your list with the rest of the class.

◀ **Canyonlands National Park, Utah**

▼ **Grand Tetons National Park, Wyoming**

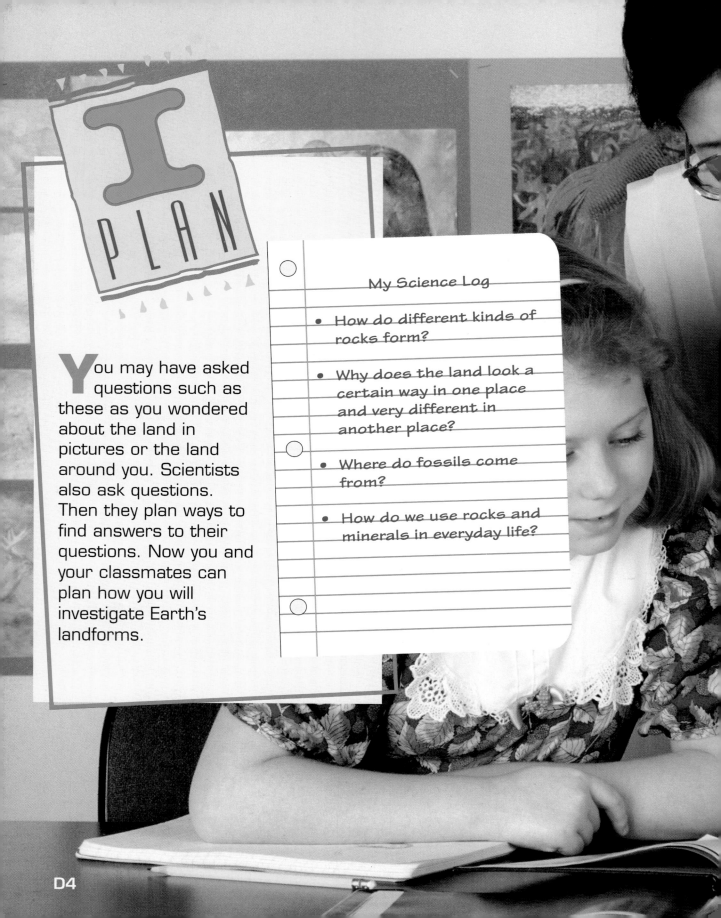

I PLAN

You may have asked questions such as these as you wondered about the land in pictures or the land around you. Scientists also ask questions. Then they plan ways to find answers to their questions. Now you and your classmates can plan how you will investigate Earth's landforms.

My Science Log

- How do different kinds of rocks form?

- Why does the land look a certain way in one place and very different in another place?

- Where do fossils come from?

- How do we use rocks and minerals in everyday life?

With Your Class

Plan how your class will use the activities and readings from the **I Investigate** part of this unit.

On Your Own

There are many ways to learn about Earth and its landforms. Following are some things you can do to explore Earth's landforms by yourself or with some classmates. Some explorations may take longer than others. Look over the suggestions and choose...

- **Projects to Do**
- **People to Contact**
- **Books to Read**

PROJECTS TO DO

ROCK COLLECTING

Rocks can tell you a lot about the history of the land. You just have to know how to "read" them. What can the rocks in your area tell you? Start a classroom rock collection. Everyone in your class should bring a few rocks to school. Use the appearance of the rocks to put them into different groups. Then use a book on rocks and minerals to find out the kinds of rocks you have. What kinds of rocks are common where you live? What do the rocks tell you about where you live?

FINDING YOUR WAY

How much do you notice about the land around you each day? Test yourself. Draw a map that shows how to get from your school to another place in town. Everyone in class should show how to get to the same place. On the map, you may show when to go straight ahead, left, or right. But don't show street names or addresses. Show landforms or natural objects (such as a hill or a big oak tree) or objects people have made (a white fence or a bus shelter). See how much you can remember about the landscape. When you finish, share your map and compare it with your classmates' maps.

PEOPLE TO CONTACT

IN PERSON

How has the land in your area changed over the years? To find out, talk to someone who has lived in your area a long time. The person can be a relative, a friend, or a neighbor. How was the land different when he or she was your age? Were there woods or swamps that no longer exist? Did your school or house exist? If not, what was on the land? Record your interview for the class.

- Friends of the Earth
- National Audubon Society
- National Park Service
- Sierra Club
- U.S. Environmental Protection Agency
- U.S. Geological Survey

BY TELEPHONE

The land is an important resource. Many government agencies and private groups work to preserve the land so that people can enjoy its beauty. They also work to make sure that plants and animals that live on the land are protected. You can call some of these agencies and groups for information. Some of them will send you materials in the mail.

BY COMPUTER

Use a computer with a modem to connect to on-line services or bulletin boards. You can look for environmental news from around the world. You can also "talk" with others to find out what the land is like where they live.

BOOKS TO READ

The Rock

by Peter Parnall (Macmillan, 1991), Outstanding Science Trade Book. The rock was huge and gave shelter to many plants and animals. Trees grew there. Animals came to eat, to hide, and to hunt. There was a pond where animals came to drink. When the fire came, the rock changed. At first it was bare except for ashes. But nature restored it so the plants and animals returned. For centuries the rock stood firm. The book explains how nature continues.

Earth Alive!

by Sandra Markle (Lothrop, Lee & Shepard, 1991). In this book, you will see how Earth is always changing. It boils, melts, and crumbles. It is moved by air and water, so it slides, flies, and explodes. Some changes take place suddenly, and some take millions of years. Look around and think about it. The Earth is exciting, dangerous, and beautiful.

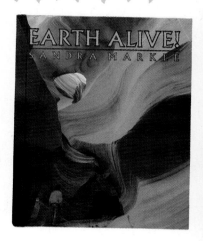

More Books to Read

The Big Rock

by Bruce Hiscock (Atheneum, 1988), Outstanding Science Trade Book. The rock in the mountains will last a long time. It has been part of Earth's crust for billions of years. This book will show you how the rock began. There were ancient seas, and then earthquakes that formed mountains. The mountains eroded. The glaciers came, and the force of the ice carried the rock away and left it where it is now.

Rocks and Soil

by Joy Richardson (Franklin Watts, 1992). The large, color photographs in this book help explain the world beneath your feet. You'll learn about Earth's crust, soil, minerals, rocks, and crystals. How do we use the treasures of the Earth? How do we find out about the past? It's all told in this book.

The Sun, the Wind and the Rain

by Lisa Westberg Peters (Henry Holt, 1988), Outstanding Science Trade Book. On the beach, Elizabeth builds a mountain out of sand. Read this book to find out how the wind and rain wear it away, just like a real mountain. The ocean washes away another one she builds, just as the cliff she walks on is being washed slowly away, too.

The Village of Round and Square Houses

by Ann Grifalconi (Little, Brown, 1986), Caldecott Honor Book. This story is based on something that really happened in a village in central Africa. In this village, some people live in one square house while others live in one round house. It was not always this way. Before the volcano erupted, life was different. This story will tell you why it changed.

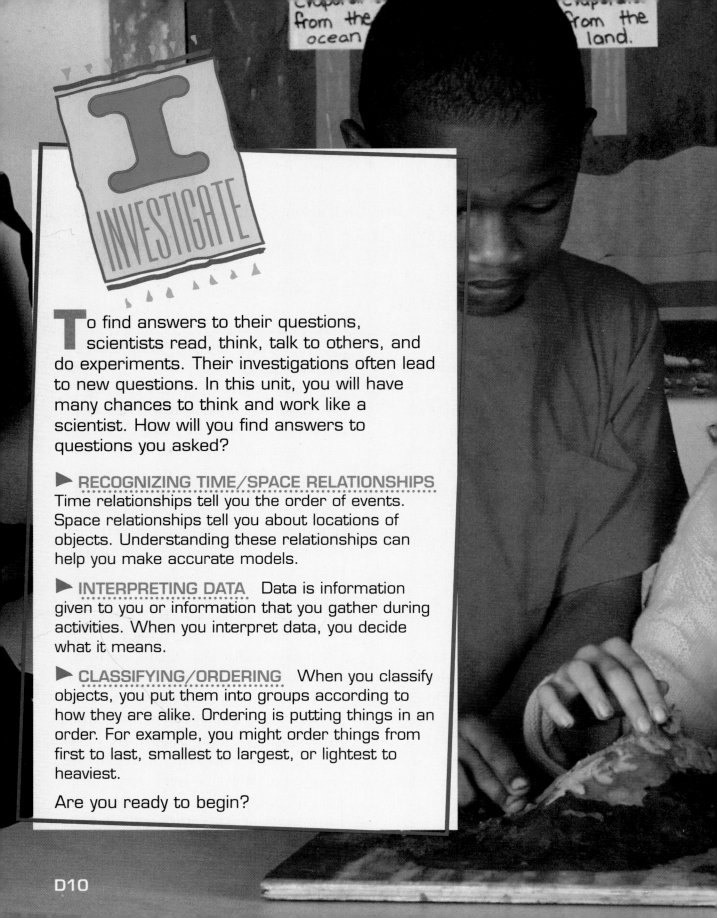

I INVESTIGATE

To find answers to their questions, scientists read, think, talk to others, and do experiments. Their investigations often lead to new questions. In this unit, you will have many chances to think and work like a scientist. How will you find answers to questions you asked?

▶ **RECOGNIZING TIME/SPACE RELATIONSHIPS** Time relationships tell you the order of events. Space relationships tell you about locations of objects. Understanding these relationships can help you make accurate models.

▶ **INTERPRETING DATA** Data is information given to you or information that you gather during activities. When you interpret data, you decide what it means.

▶ **CLASSIFYING/ORDERING** When you classify objects, you put them into groups according to how they are alike. Ordering is putting things in an order. For example, you might order things from first to last, smallest to largest, or lightest to heaviest.

Are you ready to begin?

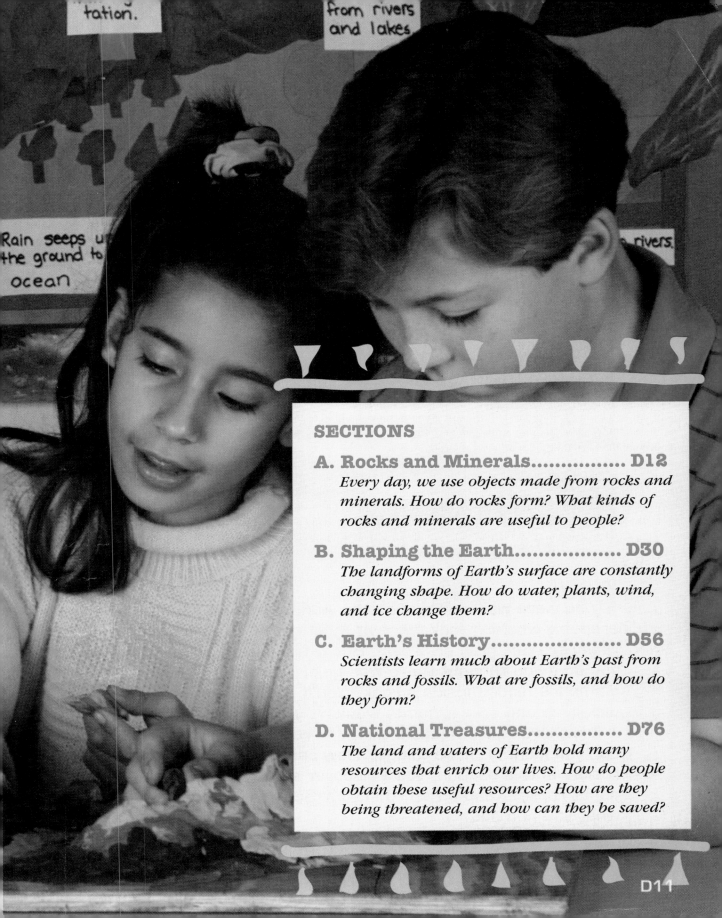

SECTIONS

SECTION A
Rocks and Minerals

If you were walking through the woods, you probably wouldn't look twice at most rocks. Many are dull gray or brown. But what would you do if you thought there was gold, silver, or diamonds hidden inside a rock? You'd be sure to pick it up and take it home, wouldn't you?

Are there really valuable things in rocks? How can you identify these things? How can people use rocks? In this section, you'll discover some things about rocks. Keep a record in your Science Log of what you find out.

▲ **Gold ore**

1 EXPLORING ROCKS AND MINERALS

Have you ever collected rocks? Or have you seen someone else's collection? What makes rocks different from one another? In this lesson, you'll investigate rocks. You'll see how different kinds of rocks form. You'll see how rocks can change. You'll also investigate some materials that make up rocks.

▼ Granite

Kinds of Rocks

If rocks could talk, each one would tell a different story. Let's take a hike into the Grand Canyon to learn the stories of some rocks.

Igneous Rocks

You're at the bottom of the Grand Canyon. The canyon is deep enough to swallow a building with 500 floors. The water of the Colorado River smashes against hard rocks. The rocks are extremely old— almost half as old as Earth itself!

These rocks are granite. You see that they have many sparkling flakes in them. But if you could have seen the rocks millions of years ago, you wouldn't have recognized them. At that time, they were red-hot and melted. Over a long time, they slowly cooled and became granite.

Rocks that start out as red-hot liquids are called **igneous** (IHG nee uhs) **rocks.** *Igneous* is a word that means "fire." So you can think of igneous rocks as "fire rocks."

Granite may form cliffs and mountains, such as these being enjoyed by a rock climber. ▶

Sedimentary Rocks

Millions of years ago, there was no Grand Canyon. At that time, an ocean covered the land. Rivers that ran into the ocean carried sand and other bits of rock. These materials, called *sediments* (SED uh muhnts), settled on the ocean floor. So did the remains of sea creatures. As time passed, more and more sediments piled up, in layer upon layer. The weight of the layers squeezed the sediments. Chemicals in the sediments cemented them together. Eventually, the squeezing and the cementing hardened the sediments into layers of rock.

As you climb upward in the Grand Canyon, you see the layers of rock. One of them is a reddish brown. It's called *sandstone*. Sandstone belongs to a second type of rock, called sedimentary (sed uh MEN tuhr ee) rocks. Sedimentary rocks are formed when sediments harden.

Sandstone is a sedimentary rock. ▶

▲ Sandstone can also form cliffs and mountains. Sandstone can be shaped by water, such as the Colorado River.

Metamorphic Rocks

Sometimes rocks that have already formed get buried deep within the Earth. Forces within the Earth squeeze the rocks from many directions. At the same time, heat from deep inside the Earth makes these rocks very hot, but it does not melt them. The squeezing and the heat change these rocks from one kind into another.

At the bottom of the Grand Canyon, you might see dark gray rocks called *slate*. Slate is one type of metamorphic (met uh MAWR fik) rock. *Metamorphic* means "changed." All metamorphic rocks form from other rocks. Slate is a metamorphic rock because it formed from a rock called *shale*. Igneous, sedimentary, and even other metamorphic rocks can be changed by heat and squeezing to form new metamorphic rocks.

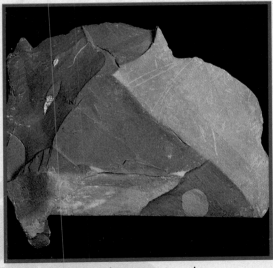

▲ Shale is a sedimentary rock.

Slate is the metamorphic rock formed from shale. ▼

THINK ABOUT IT

How could a metamorphic rock become an igneous rock?

The Rock Cycle

As you explore the Grand Canyon, you find all sorts of rocks. Some are soft and crumble between your fingers. Others are hard and have sharp edges. Some look as if they're made up of small rocks glued together. Others seem to be made of a single substance.

No matter what the rocks look like today, you can be sure that at one time they looked different. That's because rocks change as time passes.

A cycle is a group of changes that take place over and over again. This diagram of the rock cycle shows how materials that make up rocks are used again and again.

You've read about three different types of rocks—igneous, sedimentary, and metamorphic. You can see in the diagram of the rock cycle how these types of rocks are related.

In the diagram, find the arrows with the words *heat and pressure* on them. The heat comes from inside the Earth. The pressure comes from the weight of rocks pressing on other rocks. All types of rocks can be changed by heat and pressure. What kinds of rocks shown in the diagram can become metamorphic rocks?

Next, find the arrows with *wearing away by water and wind* written on them. This process forms sediments. When pressure is applied to sediments, sedimentary rocks form. What kinds of rocks can become sedimentary rocks?

Now, find the three arrows with *melting* written on them. When heat causes rocks to melt, the substances in them may change and recombine. What kinds of rocks shown in the diagram can become red-hot melted rock?

The rock cycle shows that Earth recycles its rock materials. They just keep changing from one kind of rock into another.

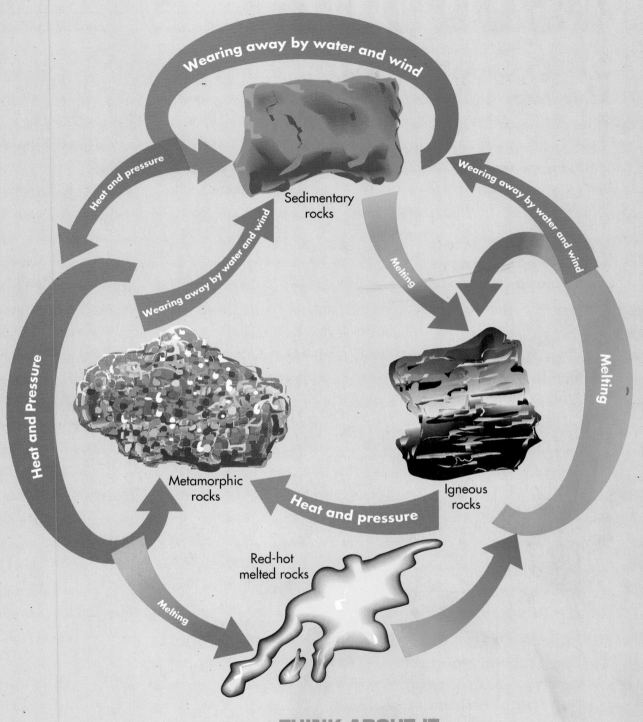

Wearing away by water and wind

Heat and pressure

Sedimentary rocks

Wearing away by water and wind

Melting

Wearing away by water and wind

Heat and Pressure

Melting

Metamorphic rocks

Heat and pressure

Igneous rocks

Melting

Red-hot melted rocks

THINK ABOUT IT

Explain why the rock cycle is a cycle.

Stories in Rocks

The rocks around you tell a story. They tell what the land around you was like long ago. The land may have been very different from what it is now. Maybe it was under an ocean. Maybe a volcano once poured hot, melted rock on the land. Maybe the rocks you playfully kick today were once deep inside the Earth. See if you can discover the story of the land around you.

DO THIS

❶ Look at the three labeled rocks. Observe them with and without the hand lens. Each rock has a letter on it. *M* stands for *metamorphic*, *S* for *sedimentary*, and *I* for *igneous*.

❷ Examine each of the mystery rocks. Compare them with the labeled rocks.

MATERIALS

- 3 labeled rocks
- 3 numbered mystery rocks
- hand lens
- Science Log data sheet

❸ Record the number of each mystery rock. Next to the number, write the letter of the labeled rock that the mystery rock is most like.

THINK AND WRITE

1. What do the mystery rocks seem to tell you about the land they came from? What events might have formed these rocks?

2. CLASSIFYING/ORDERING Sometimes putting things in order or classifying them helps you learn about them or find them for later observations. In this investigation, you classified mystery rocks by comparing them with rocks you knew about. Did this help you gather data about the rocks? Why or why not?

ACTIVITY

Identifying Minerals

What are rocks made of? All rocks are made of one or more minerals. A diamond is a mineral. A chunk of quartz, which is like a big piece of hardened sand, is also a mineral. A diamond and a chunk of quartz look very similar. How could you tell them apart? You could do it if you tested their hardness. That's because every mineral has a specific hardness. How can you find out the hardness of a mineral? Do the following activity to find out.

▲ Which is the diamond? ▲

MATERIALS
- chalk
- copper wire
- iron nail
- other materials of varying hardness
- mineral kit
- Science Log data sheet

DO THIS

1 Make a chart like the one shown.

SCRATCH–TEST RESULTS		
Material to Be Tested	**Materials It Scratches**	**Materials That Scratch It**
Chalk		
Copper Wire		
Iron Nail		

2 Try to scratch the chalk, wire, and nail with your fingernail.

3 Try to scratch all the materials with each other.

4 Choose three other materials to test for hardness. Add them to your chart.

5 On your chart, record which materials scratched which.

6 List the materials from the hardest to the softest. This will create a hardness scale.

7 Test each material, and decide where it fits in the hardness scale.

THINK AND WRITE

1. Which material was the hardest? What evidence do you have for your answer?

2. Which material was the softest? What evidence do you have for your answer?

3. How would your hardness scale help you classify rocks and minerals?

4. **INTERPRETING DATA** You collected data in this activity. You also interpreted the data. What senses did you use? How did you interpret the data you collected?

LESSON 1 REVIEW

1 Some islands are volcanoes that rise from the bottom of the ocean. What kinds of rocks would you find on the islands when they first form?

2 If you found a piece of sedimentary rock on a mountain, what would this tell you about the land?

3 Only another diamond can scratch a diamond. So what can you say about diamonds?

2 USING ROCKS AND MINERALS

Many of Earth's rocks are treasure chests. Within them, you might find the materials to make a brass trumpet, a sports car, or a jet airplane.

You Use Rocks Every Day

Some rocks contain metals, such as aluminum, iron, and nickel. These metals can be separated from the rocks. Then they can be used to make trumpets, sports cars, jet airplanes, and a lot of other things. You might be surprised at how many ways you use rocks. In fact, your life would be very different without them.

Copper comes from rocks. The pennies in your pocket have copper in them. Without copper, you wouldn't have electric lights in your home or be able to watch TV, because copper is used to make the wires that carry electricity. Copper can be combined with zinc, another metal, to form brass. Brass is used to make some instruments. ▶

Calcopyrite, shown here, contains copper. ▶

Aluminum comes from a type of mineral called *bauxite* (BAWKS yt). Aluminum is used to make cans, pots and pans, airplanes, rockets, and lightweight ladders. ▶

Bauxite ▶

◀ What does a sports car have to do with rocks? Many of the parts of cars are made of steel, and iron is used to make steel. Iron comes from a type of rock called *hematite* (HEM uh tyt).

Hematite ▶

Sometimes rocks are used pretty much as they are. Buildings may be made of blocks of rock, such as granite. Some of the world's greatest statues are made of the rock called *marble*. Gemstones need only to be cut and polished to make beautiful jewelry. ▶

THINK ABOUT IT

Explain three ways you use rocks.

ACTIVITY

Rock Hunt

Lots of things in and around your home, school, and community are made from rocks and minerals. Let's see how many of these things you can find and classify.

DO THIS

1 Make a chart like this one to record your findings. Put the chart on the clipboard.

ROCK HUNT			
Object	Where I Saw It	Use	Classification

2 Look around your home, school, or community for objects made from rocks or from materials that came from rocks.

3 When you see an object that you think was made from rocks or a rock material, write its name under the word *Object*. In the next two columns, write where you saw the object and what it's used for.

4 Classify each object. You can classify things by how they are used. For example, one group might be jewelry. Another group might be things used in construction. Still another group could be things used in transportation. Or you can make up your own groups.

THINK AND WRITE

1. Which objects are made from things taken out of rocks?

2. Which objects are made of things that still look like rocks?

3. Look over your chart. Which group has the most objects in it? Explain why the objects in this group are important to you.

4. CLASSIFYING/ORDERING In this investigation, you classified some objects made from rocks. The groups were based on the uses of things made from rocks. In what other ways might you have classified these objects?

Stone Art

If you want a message to last a long time, carve it in stone. What kinds of messages might these be? Imagine taking trips to three places to find out.

Mount Rushmore

You're a tourist visiting Mount Rushmore, a hill of granite in the Black Hills of South Dakota. You see an awesome sight—four huge faces carved in the mountain side. The faces are those of four American presidents—Washington, Jefferson, Lincoln, and Theodore Roosevelt.

Suppose you came from a time far in the future. When you looked at the faces on Mount Rushmore, what would you think? What message would you get?

The Maya

A team of scientists walks through a thick forest in Guatemala. Suddenly, the trees thin out. There is a clearing ahead. As the scientists enter the clearing, they see a huge building made of rock. And they know they have found the lost city of Tikal.

Tikal was one of many cities built by a people called the *Maya*. Most Maya lived in what is now Guatemala and Mexico. Their cities are at least a thousand years old.

The Maya were very good at science and engineering. They used limestone, a sedimentary rock, to make buildings called *pyramids*. The pyramid at Tikal is as tall as a 15-floor apartment house. The Maya used the pyramids for religious ceremonies.

Near the pyramids, the scientists find a piece of stone about the size of a person. The Maya carved all sorts of pictures in the stone. The pictures form a kind of calendar and diary. The scientists will try to figure out what stories the pictures tell. What kinds of things do you think the stories might be about?

Homes of Rock

The two cowboys shivered. An icy wind blew through the red-sandstone canyon in Colorado. The month was December. The year was 1888.

Snow covered most of the sandstone around the cowboys. But every now and then, a gust of wind would sweep the snow off the rocks. All of a sudden, one gust cleared a large area. Then the cowboys saw something they had never seen before. They stared at the ruins of houses that seemed to climb up the steep cliffs.

Thousands of people once lived in these houses. These early Americans are known as the *Anasazi* (an ah SAHZ ee). But between 600 and 700 years ago, the Anasazi left their homes. Why? Scientists suggest two reasons. Maybe the land became too dry for crops, such as corn, to grow. Or maybe other Native American people attacked the Anasazi and forced them to leave.

Today many tourists visit these cities in the cliffs. Scientists also go there to try to solve the mysteries of the Anasazi.

THINK ABOUT IT

What are three ways people in the Americas have left records of history in stone? What kinds of stone records do you think people today leave?

Maria Martinez
She Turned Rocks into Art

You have learned that you use rocks in many ways. Other people use rocks in ways you may not have thought of. Read about Maria Martinez, a Navaho potter, who used rocks in a very interesting manner.

If you were to look at the ground near the town of San Ildefonso (SAHN eel day FAHN soh) in New Mexico, you might see brown chunks of clay. In another place, you might see some dark ash that fell from a volcano long ago. You might think that both the clay and the ash were good for nothing. But to Maria Martinez, these pieces of rock were the stuff from which fine works of art could be made.

Maria Martinez was one of the great Native American makers of pottery. She made beautiful jars, bowls, and pitchers.

Pottery is made from clay, water, and materials like ash from volcanoes. When the mixture is soft and wet, it can be made into many different shapes. It is then dried, painted, and put in an oven to harden.

Maria Martinez's people had made pottery for hundreds of years. During her long life, Maria Martinez learned how to make pottery as her people had done in the past. But she also used her imagination to make new and beautiful designs.

QUICK CHECK

LESSON 2 REVIEW

❶ What are some ways you use rocks or things made from rocks in your everyday life?

❷ Name three ways that rocks and things made from rocks make your life better.

DOUBLE CHECK

SECTION A REVIEW

1. People use steel tools to carve statues. If you had a choice of carving a statue from chalk or diamond, which would you choose? Why?

2. Why are some rocks better than wood for building houses?

SECTION B
Shaping the Earth

In the western part of the United States, the jagged tops of the Rocky Mountains may be covered with snow all year round. As you travel east, the land changes. The Great Plains of the Midwest are as flat as a tabletop. The mountains of the South and East are covered with trees and other plants.

This is what the land of the United States looks like today. But it didn't always look like this, and in the future, it will look different than it does today. The land is constantly changing. What makes it change? How can a mountain grow old? How does a valley form? How can huge blocks of rocks become dusty sand? As you explore this section, you will find some answers. In your Science Log, keep a record of what you discover.

1 LANDFORMS AND MAPS

Do you have a globe in your classroom? Do some of the land parts feel rough and bumpy? What do you think these bumpy places are supposed to be? You know that land looks different in different places. Why is this so? Parts of land are high, like hills and mountains. Some parts of the Earth are very flat, like the plains found in the middle of the United States. How do mountains form? Why does Earth's surface vary so much? The following pages will give you a clue.

Earth's Landforms

To understand differences in the land, you need to look at the structure of the Earth. Let's look at that structure.

Earth is made up of layers. The outer layer of Earth, the *crust,* is only a few kilometers thick. Below the crust is a layer called the *mantle.* Below the mantle are two more layers. The *outer core* is a layer of liquid metal, and the *inner core* is a solid ball of iron and nickel.

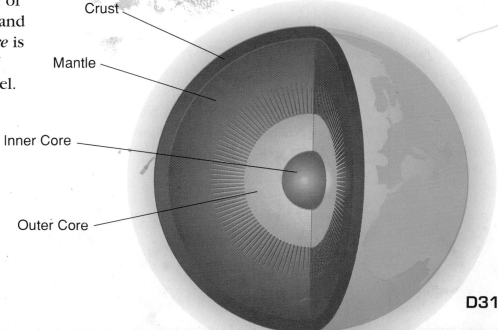

Crust

Mantle

Inner Core

Outer Core

Earth's **landforms** are features that can be seen on Earth's crust. *Mountains* are landforms that rise very high above the land around them. The low areas between the mountains are called *valleys.* Rivers are often found at the bottom of valleys. These rivers form valleys as rain flows downward from steep mountain slopes.

▲ These mountains at Glacier National Park are so high that they're covered with snow most of the year. The valley below is green with plants.

Wide, flat areas of land are called *plains*. Soil in the plains is usually good enough for crops to be grown there. A *plateau* is also a flat area, but it rises above the land around it. It looks like a mountain with the top cut off.

Compare the types of landforms shown here. How are they like the landforms where you live? How are they different?

▲ The land of the Colorado Plateau is like a tabletop.

▲ The Great Plains of the Midwest are flat and ideal for growing crops. This is where most of the country's farmland is located.

THINK ABOUT IT

Not many crops are grown on plateaus. Why not?

ACTIVITY

Folds in Earth's Crust

Heat and pressure from below Earth's crust can affect surface landforms. To see this for yourself, try this activity.

MATERIALS
- 4 paper towels (single sheets)
- water
- Science Log data sheet

DO THIS

❶ Stack the four paper towels on a table. Fold the stack in half.

❷ Carefully dampen the paper towels with water.

❸ Put your hands on the edges of the damp paper. Very slowly push the edges of the wet paper towels toward the center.

THINK AND WRITE

1. What happened as you pushed the damp paper towels?

2. Compare the area of the paper towels before you pushed them and after you pushed them.

3. Compare the height of the paper towels before you pushed them and after you pushed them.

Looking Back In this activity, the layers of paper towels stood for layers of rock that make up part of Earth's crust. When you pushed the edges of the paper towels together, the layers bent and folded. Part of the "crust" became higher than the "land" around it. This is similar to what has happened in some places on Earth. Some mountains have formed over a very long period of time as pieces of crust and mantle collided with other pieces of crust and mantle. Areas of folded rock formed the Appalachian Mountains. Other mountains formed when forces on rock layers caused them to break and one part was pushed up. Still other mountains formed because of volcanoes.

A Slice of Rock

To learn more about different landforms, you can look at a map. Many of the maps that you've seen show highways and roads. But there are also maps that show the structures of landforms.

One type of map is called a *cross-section map*. This map shows the rock layers inside a landform. It is similar to what you would see if you sliced into a layer cake and looked inside. If the rock layers have been folded, the folding will show on this kind of map. Cross-section maps, like all other maps, have a scale. A scale shows how the distance on a map compares to the real distance on Earth.

A cross-section map also shows the elevation of a landform. *Elevation,* or the height of the land, is measured from a beginning point called sea level. **Sea level** is the average level of the sea where it meets the land. Suppose a mountain has an elevation of 4,200 meters (13,779 feet). This means it rises 4,200 meters above sea level.

THINK ABOUT IT

Look at the cross-section map. What is the elevation of the mountain?

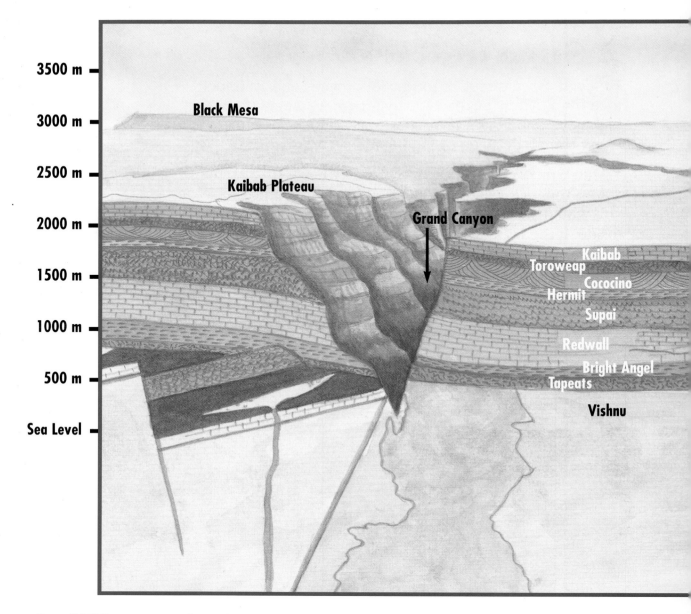

Scale labels (left axis): 3500 m, 3000 m, 2500 m, 2000 m, 1500 m, 1000 m, 500 m, Sea Level

Labels: Black Mesa, Kaibab Plateau, Grand Canyon, Kaibab, Toroweap, Cococino, Hermit, Supai, Redwall, Bright Angel, Tapeats, Vishnu

A Slice of the Grand Canyon

Now let's take a look at a cross-section map of a
famous landform—the Grand Canyon. The Grand Canyon
is a beautiful landform located in Arizona. A canyon is
actually a very deep, steep-sided valley formed by a
river. Try to answer the questions as you look at the
cross-section map of the Grand Canyon.

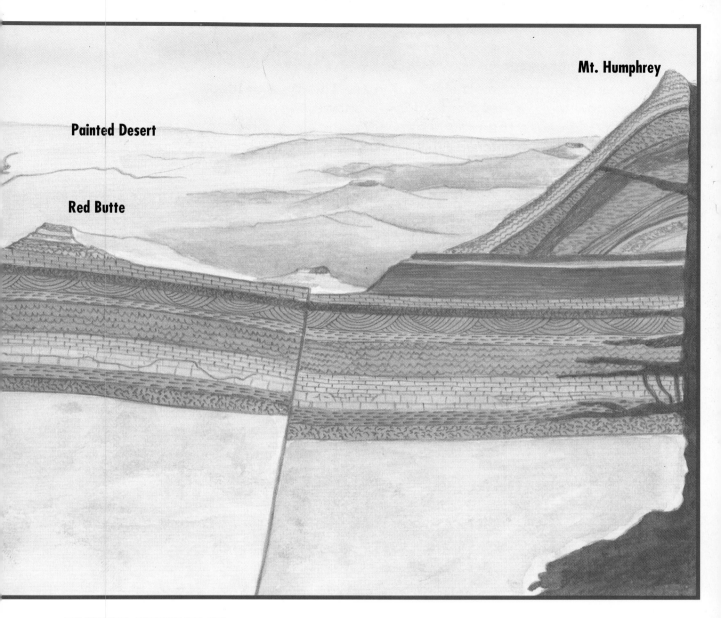

Painted Desert

Red Butte

Mt. Humphrey

THINK ABOUT IT

1. The bottom of the Grand Canyon cuts deep into the ground. But it is still above sea level. What is the elevation of the bottom of the Grand Canyon?

2. What is the elevation of Mount Humphrey?

3. Your car stops near Red Butte, and you decide to climb it. You want the climb to be as easy as possible. Which side of Red Butte do you climb? Why?

Visiting the Grand Canyon

Another useful map is an elevation map. This type of map shows how high or low the land is—it shows *elevation*. However, because the map is flat, different elevations are shown in different colors. Which color shows high elevation?

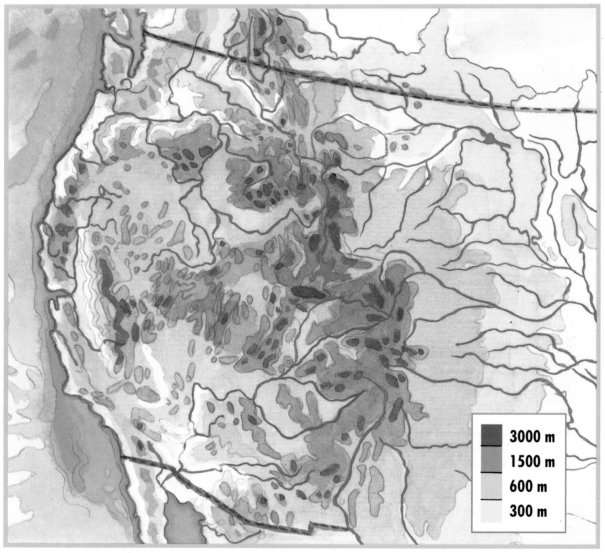

	3000 m
	1500 m
	600 m
	300 m

   Suppose you and your family arrive at the Visitor Center at the Grand Canyon National Park. A park ranger gives you a map that shows the elevation of areas in and around the canyon. You begin to plan a trip through the canyon. As you think about your trip, some questions pop into your mind. You study the map in search of the answers.

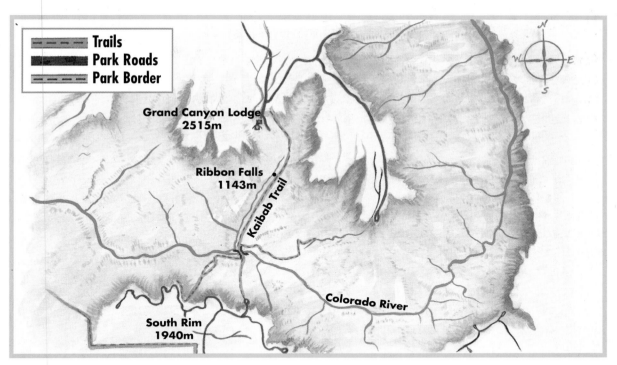

Trails
Park Roads
Park Border

Grand Canyon Lodge
2515m

Ribbon Falls
1143m

Kaibab Trail

Colorado River

South Rim
1940m

You decide to take a helicopter ride across the Grand Canyon from south to north, following the Kaibab Trail. Will the elevation be the same where you land as where you take off? How do you know?

Down the trail, you see the Phantom Ranch suspension bridge. What does the bridge cross?

You get to Ribbon Falls and have a picnic lunch. After lunch, you start a hike that will end at the Grand Canyon Lodge. Will you be walking downhill, uphill, or on flat land? How do you know?

When you get to the Colorado River, you change your mind about crossing the Grand Canyon. Instead, you decide to hop on a raft. In which direction will the river carry you? How do you know?

LESSON 1 REVIEW

❶ What kind of map would you use if you wanted to see the rock layers inside a mountain?

❷ When would you rather have an elevation map— when traveling across mountains or when traveling across a plain? Explain your answer.

❸ Name four landforms and draw a diagram of each one. Tell how they are alike and how they are different.

2 WEATHERING

Look at the cliff in the photograph. Notice all the broken rock at the cliff's base. Where do you think the rock came from? In this lesson, you'll find some answers.

Physical Weathering

You've already read about landforms. You've probably realized that landforms are made from rock. You've also read that landforms change over time. Since landforms change over time, it makes sense that the rocks that help make up the landforms also change. You learned some ways rocks change when you studied the rock cycle in the last section. In what other ways do you think rocks change?

Any process that causes rocks to break down is called **weathering.** Weathering is caused by water, wind, ice, plants, and other factors.

When the weather is warm, water seeps into the cracks in rocks. If the temperature gets cold enough, the water turns to ice. Ice takes up more space than water does. That means that water expands when it freezes. When water expands in the cracks of rocks, it breaks the rocks apart.

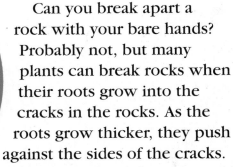

Water can freeze in the cracks of rocks and break the rocks apart. ▶

Plant roots can break large rocks into small pieces. ▼

Can you break apart a rock with your bare hands? Probably not, but many plants can break rocks when their roots grow into the cracks in the rocks. As the roots grow thicker, they push against the sides of the cracks. They push so hard that they break the rock open. This is another way that big rocks get smaller. The breaking up of rocks by water, ice, and plants is called **physical weathering.**

THINK ABOUT IT

How can water change rocks?

A C T I V I T Y

Sand at Work

Rocks are weathered by water, ice, and plants. Do the following activity to discover another material that causes weathering of rocks.

DO THIS

1 Measure and record the mass of the rocks. Then measure and record the mass of the jar and the sand together.

2 Put the rocks in the jar with the sand, and fasten the lid tightly.

❸ Each day for a week, shake the jar for 30 minutes.

❹ After a week, measure and record the mass of the rocks. Also measure and record the mass of the sand and the jar.

THINK AND WRITE

1. Describe what the sandstone looked like at the beginning of the experiment. Describe what the sand looked like.

2. After a week, what happened to the sandstone? What happened to the sand? Explain your observations.

3. Compare the masses of sand and rock from steps 1 and 4.

4. INTERPRETING DATA   Use your interpretation of the data in this activity to infer what happened at a red-sand beach. Above the beach is a red-rock cliff. The beach is completely covered with red sand. Where do you think the sand came from?

Looking Back   In this activity, you observed that sand particles can wear away rock. This also happens in nature, with the help of the wind. Sand particles blown by the wind are like the particles in sandpaper. The wind blows the sand particles against rock. The rock is worn away in the same way that wood is worn away by sandpaper. This process is called *abrasion*.

Chemical Weathering

If you've ever visited a large underground cave, you might have seen what looked like stone icicles hanging from the cave's ceiling or rising from its floor. What are those odd-looking stone shapes? How and why did they form?

Chemical weathering is a process that takes place when certain chemicals act on rocks. The process that formed these stone icicles began when water dissolved the minerals in certain types of rocks. The water flowed into underground caves and dripped from the ceilings. As the water dripped, it left behind tiny bits of minerals that built up to form the pointed stone.

THINK ABOUT IT

Inside a cave, what kind of rock has weathered? What kind of chemical did the weathering?

ACTIVITY

Dissolving Rocks

Chemical weathering can take place inside a jar just as it does outside. Try the activity to find out more.

MATERIALS

- 6 clear jars or plastic cups
- wax pencil
- limestone rock chips
- sandstone rock chips
- quartzite rock chips
- water
- vinegar
- Science Log data sheet

DO THIS

❶ Use the pencil to write the word *limestone* on two of the jars. On two other jars, write *sandstone*, and on the last two jars, write *quartzite*.

❷ Put a few limestone chips in the jars labeled *limestone*. Put a few sandstone chips in the jars labeled *sandstone*. Put a few quartzite chips in the jars labeled *quartzite*.

❸ Fill one jar of each pair with water. Fill the other jar of each pair with vinegar. (Vinegar is a mild acid.)

❹ Observe and record what happens in each jar. Repeat the observation 20 minutes later and then again the next day.

THINK AND WRITE

1. Which kind of rock changed?

2. What caused the rock to change? How do you know?

3. Look at the photograph of the cave. It has stone icicles on the floor and the ceiling. What kind of rock do you think the cave is made of? Explain your answer.

4. INTERPRETING DATA You had to use the data you collected in the activity to help you answer the question about the stone icicles in the cave. What was the data? How did you interpret the data and apply it to the cave?

▲ **Elephant rock**

Looking Back Chemical weathering can also occur in other ways. The rocks in the picture are part of the Valley of Fire in Nevada. Notice that part of the rock formation is a reddish brown while some is a lighter color. The rocks didn't always look like this. Once, all the rock was the same light color. What turned part of it darker? Oxygen in the air combined with iron in the hill to make rust. Rust is soft and flaky, and it easily turns to dust.

Unusual Rock Shapes

These shapes are the results of the actions of wind, water, and ice. It took millions of years for these unusual shapes to form.

◄ Ship Rock in New Mexico is all that is left of the inside of an old volcano. It is made of a dark igneous rock called *basalt*.

This unusual shape formed when soft, easily weathered rock underneath harder rock was worn away. ▶

◄ In Death Valley, California, Mushroom Rock formed because of the wind blowing sand against the rock.

These rocks in the Black Hills of South Dakota are called *Needles*, because of their sharp points. The rocks formed when weathering occurred. ▶

◀ Soft layers of rock are worn away faster than hard layers. That's how these unusual "creatures," called *rock goblins*, formed.

LESSON 2 REVIEW

❶ Explain how desert sandstorms can weather rock.

❷ Some factories send chemicals into the air that mix with rain and form an acid. If you were building a stone house nearby, what kind of rock would you *not* use? What kinds of rock might you use? Give examples and explain.

3 EROSION

Many people have seen the Grand Canyon. They have described the stacked layers of rock as looking like pages in a book. They have told about the pink rattlesnakes that hide among the rocks. They have heard mountain lions roaring in the night. And they have seen eagles soaring through the air.

An 11-year-old Native American boy named Andrew Jones wrote a poem about his experience in the Grand Canyon. These are his words.

Canyons, Echoing
going away—coming back
repeating my voice

Andrew's voice echoed because of the steep walls of the canyon. How could such walls form?

What Is Erosion?

The process by which running water formed the Grand Canyon is called *erosion*. Look at some examples of erosion.

Erosion is the process by which weathered rock and soil are moved from one place to another. Water moving over the land and in rivers is the most effective agent of erosion. An *agent* is any force that erodes rock or soil. Other agents of erosion are waves, gravity, wind, and huge, moving sheets of ice called *glaciers*.

During erosion, weathering continues. Moving rocks bump each other and break up more. The moving rocks also wear away the rock over which they move.

▲ Waves can carry rocks and sand along a coast. The waves also pick up and smash rocks against the rocks of the shore, causing erosion.

▲ Glaciers pick up soil, rocks, and even boulders like this one and can carry them hundreds of kilometers from where they started.

Wind can move large amounts of sand from one area to another. ▼

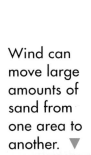

◀ Gravity pulls weathered rock and soil down hills. Erosion by gravity can cause landslides or rockslides.

THINK ABOUT IT

How do weathering and erosion work together to change landforms?

ACTIVITY

How Does Moving Water Change Land?

Of all the forces that change the land, one of the most powerful is moving water. The carrying away of weathered rock by running water is one type of erosion. Scientists have found evidence that the Colorado River carved the Grand Canyon in this way in only five million years. That means its rushing water wore away and carried off enough rock to make a canyon 2,000 meters (about 6,560 feet) deep. Not all rivers are as powerful as the Colorado. What makes one river a better carver than another? Let's find out.

MATERIALS

- large tray
- sand
- books
- pitcher
- water
- Science Log data sheet

DO THIS

1. Make a layer of sand in one half of the tray. Put one book under the end of the tray that holds the sand.

2. Slowly pour water onto the sand.

3. After a few seconds, stop pouring. Observe what happened to the sand. Draw a diagram to show what happened.

4. Repeat steps 1–3, but this time pour the water faster.

5. Repeat steps 1–3, but this time tilt the tray more by putting more books under it.

THINK AND WRITE

1. In this activity, what did the sand and the water stand for? How did the changes you made affect the flow of the water?

2. What increased the cutting power of your "river" the most?

Roads of Water

Rivers have been used by travelers all over the world. On these pages, you will learn how these roads of water form.

▲ The Colorado River moves swiftly through the Grand Canyon.

▲ In the spring, snow begins to melt high in the mountains. Drops of water splash from rock to rock. The drops come together to make little trickles of water that run downhill. A rain shower adds more water, and the trickles become a stream.

▲ The Yukon River moves slowly through Alaska and Canada.

Mountains stretch over many states. But the waters that flow down them end up in just a few great rivers. In the United States there are three mountain areas that each feed a great river. Because these areas drain water off the land, they are called *drainage basins*.

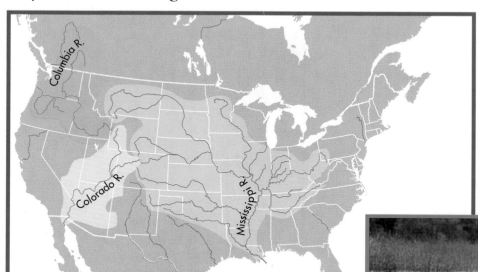

▲ Drainage basins of the Colorado, Columbia, and Mississippi rivers

The map on this page shows the drainage basins for the Colorado, Columbia, and Mississippi rivers. In some places, such as the Grand Canyon, the rivers plunge steeply downward. In other places, such as the southern part of the Mississippi, the rivers run toward the ocean over land that is almost flat.

No matter how these rivers flow, they always do the same things. They wear away parts of the land. They carry worn-away bits of rock, sand, soil, and clay wherever they go.

▲ The source of the mighty Mississippi River is so shallow you can walk across it.

As the Mississippi moves toward the Gulf of Mexico, it becomes wider and deeper. ▼

THINK ABOUT IT

How can water carve a valley?

The End of the River Road

You have seen why rivers are important agents of erosion. Now see what happens to the materials they carry away.

When rivers reach the sea, their waters slow down. They can no longer hold the bits of rock, sand, soil, and clay they have been carrying. So they begin to drop these materials.

In some places, the dumped materials pile up to make new land. This new land at a river's mouth is called a *delta*. One of the largest deltas in the world lies at the mouth of the Mississippi River, where it empties into the Gulf of Mexico. This delta looks like a huge fan. It's a fan that is 60 kilometers (37 miles) across!

◀ The Mississippi delta as it looks from space

The Mississippi delta has rich soil. ▼

Rivers don't just wear away the land. Sometimes they build up the land. The soil in deltas is very rich in nutrients. Plants that grow in the delta grow in soil that came from mountains and land hundreds of kilometers to the north.

THINK ABOUT IT

Why are rivers important to the land and to people?

Glaciers—What Are They?

Glaciers aren't things most people can see in their neighborhood. However, there have been times in Earth's history when glaciers covered much more of Earth than they do today. Read the next article to find out what glaciers are and what they do.

HUGE RIVERS of ICE

from *National Geographic World*

Listen. All is quiet as you gaze across the mountains. Below you a giant ribbon of ice winds among the rocky peaks. The ice looks firm and still—but it's on the move. How do you know? Once in a while the ground shakes slightly, and a rumble like distant thunder breaks the quiet. The ribbon of ice is actually a *river* of ice. It's a glacier. Glaciers form in parts of the world where snow piles up faster than it melts—in mountains or in other areas that stay cold most of the year. Over time, the snow crystals change to ice. When the ice is thick enough, its own weight causes it to move. Only then is it a glacier. The build-up may take a few years or hundreds of years. Once in motion, the ice creeps down a slope, perhaps traveling only an inch a day.

In Greenland and in Antarctica, glaciers called ice sheets cover thousands of square miles. Most glaciers are smaller and form on high mountains such as Alaska's Mount McKinley.

Different parts of the same glacier move at different speeds. The sides and bottom of the moving ice grind against mountain walls. These parts move more slowly than does the ice in the center. Gradually the sections pull apart and the ice cracks, forming deep canyons, or crevasses (krih VASS uhz).

A river of ice inches down a valley in the Austrian Alps. This moving ice is called a glacier. It formed over many years, as snow collected near the peaks and the crystals turned to ice. As more snow fell, the ice grew so thick that it began to move under its own weight. A glacier wears away mountainsides as it moves.

Master Mountain Carvers

A glacier changes the land. It digs out rocks and boulders, gradually carving a huge, bowl-shaped hollow called a cirque (SUHRK). As it creeps downhill, the glacier scrapes the valley floor and the mountain walls.

Continuing its slide, the glacier and the rock material along its edge grind against the mountainsides. This forms a deep, U-shaped valley that will remain long after the glacier has melted.

Icescapes

White areas on the map show glaciers around the world. Such ice spreads across one-tenth of Earth's land. It occurs on mainlands and on islands. The largest glaciers, called ice sheets, lie in polar regions—in Greenland and in Antarctica. They are about two miles thick in places.

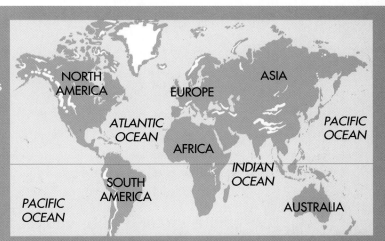

LESSON 3 REVIEW

1 Why might one river change land differently from the way another river changes land?

2 When a river overflows its banks, what kind of damage occurs?

3 How are the actions of a river and a glacier alike? How are they different?

 DOUBLE CHECK

SECTION B REVIEW

1. How do maps help people understand different landforms?

2. Tell how weathering and erosion are alike. Tell how they are different.

SECTION C
Earth's History

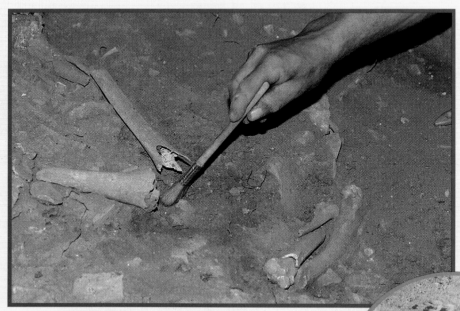

▲ **Uncovering dinosaur fossils**

Using a small brush, you slowly move away soil clinging to a large, flat rock. As you brush, you see that the rock isn't flat all over. There are dents in it. A few more strokes of the brush, and the dents take on a shape. You finally realize that you are looking at the footprint of a dinosaur!

▲ **Dinosaur footprint**

Now that you've discovered the footprint, questions race through your mind. What kind of dinosaur made the prints? What did it look like? How long ago did it live? In this section, you will learn how studying rocks and the remains of once-living things can help answer questions such as these.

1 ROCK LAYERS AND THE FOSSIL RECORD

Suppose you are looking into a bedroom with no one in it. What can you tell about whose room it is? There are many clues in the room that can give you answers. In this lesson, you'll learn that many clues found below Earth's surface can tell you about Earth's past. You've already read about how sediments can become rock over millions of years. The rock layers contain many clues that tell what the land was like when the layers were formed.

Rock Layers

Scientists gather data from Earth's surface and from beneath it. Read on to get an idea of how that happens.

To understand how people gather information from layers of rock, think how you might investigate a garbage dump. Suppose you've been asked to find out how old the garbage dump is. You've taken on the messy job of digging through the dump from top to bottom.

You use the newspapers you find in each layer of the dump to determine the age of the garbage around it. At first, you are digging through a layer of newly dumped garbage. As you dig farther down, you find a layer of garbage a year old. Even farther down is a layer that's two years old, and so on, until you reach a layer of ten-year-old garbage. The next sample is soil with no garbage. You now know that the garbage dump is ten years old.

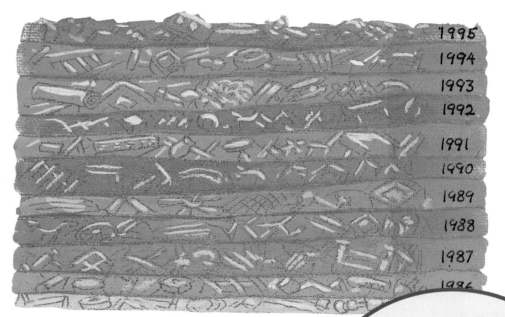

1995
1994
1993
1992
1991
1990
1989
1988
1987
1986

The rock layers of Earth's crust are laid down in much the same way as the layers of garbage in a garbage dump. Rocks are often found with one layer resting on top of another. And, like the top garbage layers, the rock layers on the top are the newest. The layers of rock get older the farther down you go.

▲ This roadbed was cut through a hill containing layers and layers of rock.

Scientists use the order of rock layers to decide how old the rock layers are. Finding the age of rocks helps scientists find out the history of plants and animals on Earth. How are rocks related to plants and animals? Fossils may be found in some rocks. A **fossil** is the preserved trace or remains of a once-living thing, usually a plant or an animal. When scientists figure out how old the rocks are, they can also figure out how long ago these organisms lived.

Sometimes scientists do just the opposite. If they know the time in history when a plant or an animal lived, that tells them how old the rock layer is.

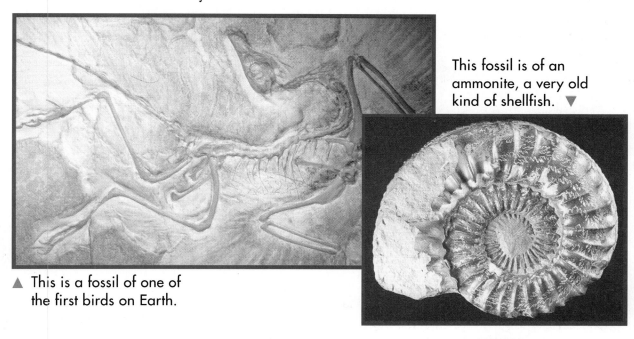

This fossil is of an ammonite, a very old kind of shellfish. ▼

▲ This is a fossil of one of the first birds on Earth.

Plants can form fossils, also, as you can see from these fossil leaves. ▶

THINK ABOUT IT

How are the newspapers in a garbage dump like the fossils in rock layers? How are they different?

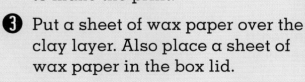

The Age of Fossils

In this activity, you and your classmates will make your own model rock layers and fossils. Then you will see if you can find out how old your classmates' fossils are.

DO THIS

❶ Make a chart like the one shown.

"ROCK" LAYERS AND "FOSSILS"		
Layer	Clay Color	Shell Number
1		
2		
3		
4		
5		

❷ Use clay of one color to make a layer on the bottom of the shoe box. Press one of the seashells into the clay to make a print. Remove the shell and mark it with a code number. Don't use code numbers that are in order, such as 1, 2, 3, 4, 5. Record the color of the clay layer and the code number of the shell used to make the print.

❸ Put a sheet of wax paper over the clay layer. Also place a sheet of wax paper in the box lid.

4 In the box lid, make a new layer out of another color of clay. Press a different shell into the top of this layer. Mark this shell with a different code number. Record the clay's color and the shell's code number.

5 Carefully put this layer over the first layer. Put a sheet of wax paper over the new layer.

6 Repeat steps 4 and 5, using all the colors of clay to make more layers and shell prints. When you finish, put your shells in the box lid.

7 Exchange your clay layers and shells with those of another group. Make a chart like the one you made at the beginning of the activity. Then remove and examine each layer of clay. Do not mix up the order of the layers. Match each shell to its print. Use your chart to record the color of the clay and the code number of the shell that made the print.

THINK AND WRITE

1. The layers of clay are model rock layers, and the shell prints are model fossils. Use what you know about rock layers to write the numbers of the shells in order from oldest to newest. Explain how you figured out the order.

2. **RECOGNIZING TIME/SPACE RELATIONSHIPS** Time relationships tell you the order of events. Space relationships tell you about locations of objects. How did you use both the time relationships of the rock layers and the space relationships of the fossils in this activity?

LESSON 1 REVIEW

How are rock layers and fossils related?

2 FOSSILS

Think back to the photo of the dinosaur footprint at the beginning of this section. Think about how the print was made. The rock it is in began as mud. The dinosaur's feet left their marks in the mud wherever the dinosaur stepped. The mud was slowly covered over. After a very, very long time, the mud was changed by heat and pressure into rock. Over time, the soil and rock above the footprint were worn away. The rock that used to be mud was exposed, revealing the print.

Fossil worm burrow ▼

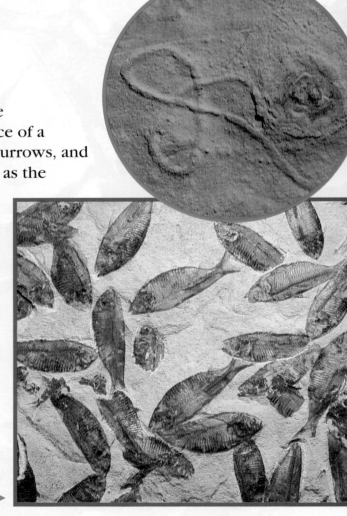

Kinds of Fossils

Fossils can be formed in several ways. Read on to find out more.

Imprints

As you have probably realized by now, the dinosaur's footprint is a fossil. It is the trace of a once-living animal. Fossils such as trails, burrows, and wormholes were formed in the same way as the footprints. They were originally made in soft dirt or mud that was later changed into rock.

These fish all died at once. Something happened to all of them, and they ended up on the bottom. The shape of their bones was pressed into the soft bottom that, over time, hardened into rock. This formed an almost flat fossil called an imprint. Common imprints are of fish, leaves, feathers, and, of course, footprints. ▶

Molds and Casts

The animal that lived in this shell died a long time ago. The shell fell to the bottom of the ocean. Mud quickly covered the shell. Over a very long time, the mud changed into rock around the shell. Water seeping through the rock dissolved the shell. Left behind in the rock layer was a space that had the shape of the shell. A space left behind in hardened material is a kind of fossil called a *mold*. But the process did not stop. Sometimes a mold fills with minerals that harden. The minerals take the shape of the living thing or the part of a living thing that was buried. A filled-in mold is a kind of fossil called a *cast*. The photograph shows the cast of a sea animal called a *trilobite* (TRY loh byt).

▲ This shellfish fossil looks just like the outside of the real thing!

▲ This trilobite fossil is a cast.

D63

Dinosaurs lived on Earth more than 65 million years ago. But scientists know a lot about these animals because they have found their bones. Bones of once-living things, such as dinosaurs, are usually casts, although they can form in the same way as petrified (PEH trih fyd) wood. You'll learn about that later.

Scientists put together the fossil bones to make a skeleton. From the skeleton, scientists can make a model of a whole dinosaur. Digging up the bones is very delicate work. Each bone must be dug up separately, cleaned, and preserved. Then the bones can be put together.

◀ Scientists unearthing the bones of a dinosaur in Wyoming.

This dinosaur skeleton ▶ was found in the same area as the dig in the picture above.

Wood Fossils

This is a "forest" of stone trees called a petrified forest. *Petrify* means "turn to stone." The real trees died long ago. Water, containing minerals from rocks, seeped into the wood. As the wood slowly rotted away, the minerals took its place. The minerals hardened into stone in the shape of the wood they replaced. ▼

Preserved in Sap, Ice, or Tar

This insect is millions of years old. It got stuck in the sap of a tree. The sap hardened into a fossil called *amber*. The whole insect was preserved inside. You can even see its wings. ▶

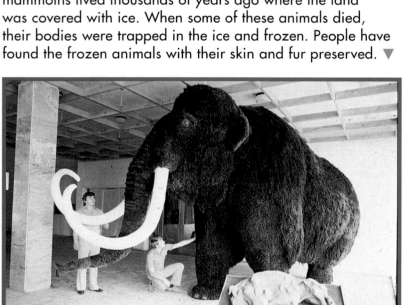

Whole animals can also be preserved in ice. Woolly mammoths lived thousands of years ago where the land was covered with ice. When some of these animals died, their bodies were trapped in the ice and frozen. People have found the frozen animals with their skin and fur preserved. ▼

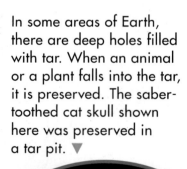

In some areas of Earth, there are deep holes filled with tar. When an animal or a plant falls into the tar, it is preserved. The saber-toothed cat skull shown here was preserved in a tar pit. ▼

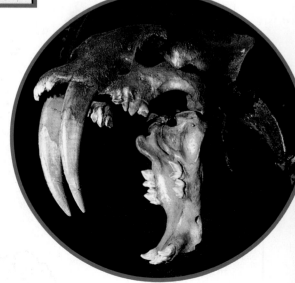

THINK ABOUT IT

1. How are the fossils that are found in amber, in tar, and in ice alike?

2. How are molds and imprints the same? How are they different?

Fossils: Clues to the Past

Scientists and teachers may use many words to explain how fossils help you understand Earth's history. A poet often uses far fewer words to tell you the same thing. Read this poem to learn more about fossils.

FOSSILS

by Lilian Moore

Older than
books,
than scrolls,

older
than the first
tales told

or the
first words
spoken

are the stories

in forests that
turned to
stone

in ice walls
that trapped the
mammoth

in the long
bones of
dinosaurs—

the fossil
stories that begin
Once upon a time

THINK ABOUT IT

What does the poem tell you about fossils?

Riddle of the Grand Canyon

You've discovered that by studying rock layers, you can solve riddles about what the land was like a long time ago. In a similar way, fossils can help scientists solve riddles about things that lived a long time ago.

The drawing shows layers of rock found in the Grand Canyon and fossils found in the layers. Both the rocks and the fossils are clues to the history of the Grand Canyon. Look at the drawing and read the captions. Then answer the questions to find out how good a scientific detective you are.

1. What is the oldest layer of rock?

2. What is the youngest layer of rock?

3. What do the kinds of fossils found in the Toroweap Formation and Kaibab Limestone tell you about the history of the Grand Canyon?

4. Which animals probably lived on Earth first, sharks or brachiopods? What evidence supports your answer?

Kaibab limestone
Fossils of sharks, sponges, and sea lilies

Toroweap formation
Fossils of corals and animals called *brachiopods* that looked like clams

Coconino sandstone
Fossils of reptiles and scorpions
Rocks that look like hardened sand dunes

Hermit shale
Fossil of a large amphibian that lived in swamps
Fossils of ferns and insects

Supai formation
Fossils of plants and primitive reptiles that lived in swamps

Redwall limestone
Fossils of brachiopods found here as well as in the Toroweap formation

Bright angel shale
Fossils of small sea animals found here

Tapeats sandstone
Fossil algae

Vishnu schist
No fossils here
Igneous rocks cut through this layer.

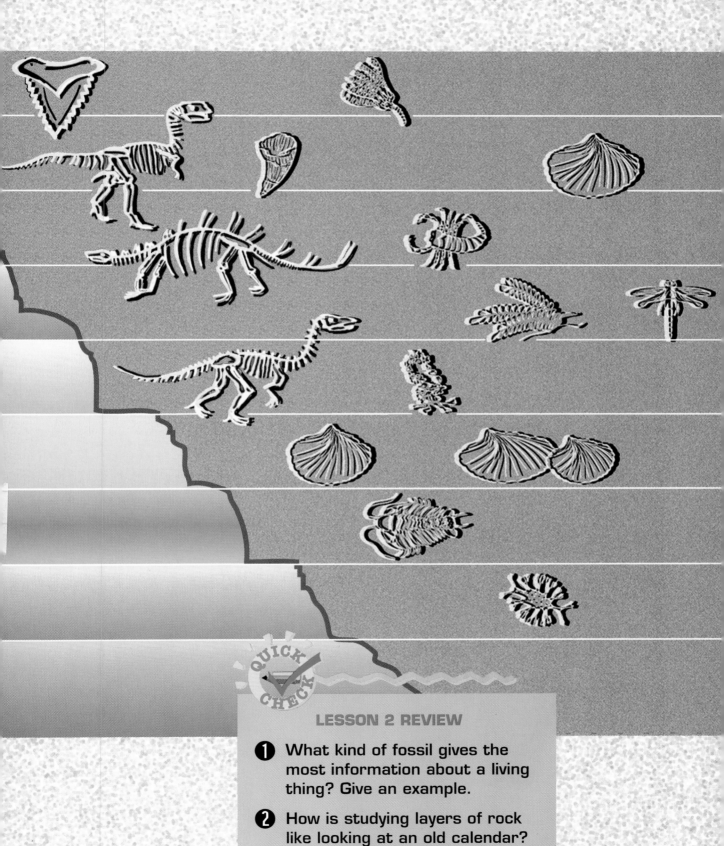

LESSON 2 REVIEW

❶ What kind of fossil gives the most information about a living thing? Give an example.

❷ How is studying layers of rock like looking at an old calendar?

3 GEOLOGIC TIME

How long is a long time ago? To your grandfather, a long time ago is when he was in fourth grade. To a fourth-grade student, a long time ago is when he or she was in first grade. To a dinosaur expert, a long time ago is when dinosaurs still lived on Earth. In this lesson, you will learn about Earth's history. It describes what has happened since the Earth formed a very, very, very long time ago.

Cryptozoic Eon	Phanerozoic Eon					
	Paleozoic Era					
Precambrian or Hadean, Archean, and Proterozoic Eras	**Cambrian Period 570-505 million years ago**	**Ordovician Period 505-438 million years ago**	**Silurian Period 438-408 million years ago**	**Devonian Period 408-360 million years ago**	**Carboniferous Period 360-286 million years ago**	
Beginning of Earth Seas form Mountains start to form Life begins in the sea Jellyfish appear	Continents partly covered with seas Trilobites, sponges, brachiopods evolve	Volcanoes very active Mountains grow First fish evolve	First land plants evolve Coral reefs form	New York's Acadian Mountains rise First forests evolve First insects, sharks and amphibians evolve	Appalachian Mountains rise Ice Age comes First reptiles, mosses, and insects that fly	
	Early / Middle / Late	Early / Late		Early / Middle / Late	Mississippian / Pennsylvanian	

D70

Once upon a Time . . .

About 140 million years ago, a strange animal had appeared on Earth. It had wings with claws on them and sharp teeth in its jaws. It had a long tail and looked very much like a small, flying dinosaur. You can see a picture of its fossil on page D59.

But when scientists examined the animal's fossil, they found evidence of something else—feathers! Had they discovered the first bird? That question is still under debate. How did they know it was 140 million years old? They knew because the fossil was found in rock that was 140 million years old.

The chart shows a calendar of Earth's history and some of the living things that first appeared during different parts of Earth's history.

Because Earth's history is so long, its parts are not divided into days, weeks, months, or years. The largest parts of Earth's history are divided into eras. Eras are divided into periods.

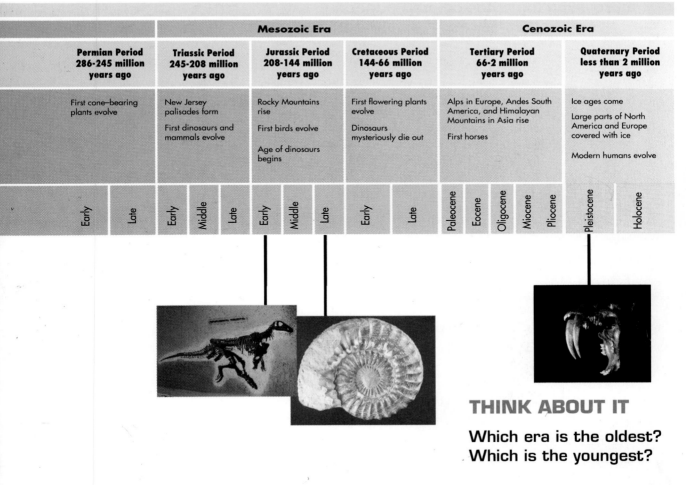

	Mesozoic Era			Cenozoic Era	
Permian Period 286-245 million years ago	**Triassic Period** 245-208 million years ago	**Jurassic Period** 208-144 million years ago	**Cretaceous Period** 144-66 million years ago	**Tertiary Period** 66-2 million years ago	**Quaternary Period** less than 2 million years ago
First cone-bearing plants evolve	New Jersey palisades form / First dinosaurs and mammals evolve	Rocky Mountains rise / First birds evolve / Age of dinosaurs begins	First flowering plants evolve / Dinosaurs mysteriously die out	Alps in Europe, Andes South America, and Himalayan Mountains in Asia rise / First horses	Ice ages come / Large parts of North America and Europe covered with ice / Modern humans evolve
Early / Late	Early / Middle / Late	Early / Middle / Late	Early / Late	Paleocene / Eocene / Oligocene / Miocene / Pliocene	Pleistocene / Holocene

THINK ABOUT IT

Which era is the oldest?
Which is the youngest?

D71

ACTIVITY

Making a Geologic Time Line

Compared with all of Earth's history, how long have fish been on Earth? During what portion of Earth's history did dinosaurs live? An easy way to answer these questions is to make a time line. In this way, you can actually *see* periods of time. Here's how you can make a chart that helps you see time.

DO THIS

❶ Measure and cut 460 cm of colored paper. Then measure and cut 460 cm of adding machine tape. Glue the adding machine tape across the top of the colored paper.

❷ At the left end of the tape, draw a line and write below it *Formation of Earth—4.6 billion years ago.*

❸ Measure 330 cm from the right side of the paper. Draw a line across the tape and label it *First organisms—3.3 billion years ago.*

4 Add the labels for *a–i* on the right. Each measurement should be made from the right side of the paper. Make drawings to illustrate your time line.

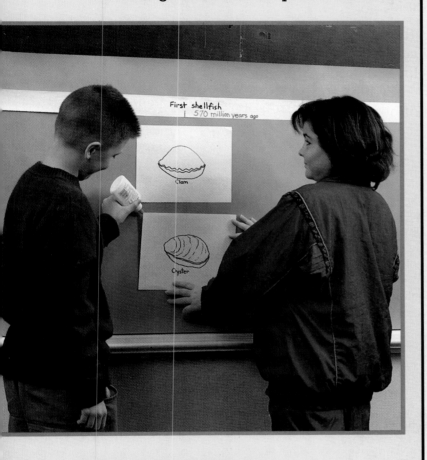

a. 57 cm: First shellfish (early animals that were like clams, oysters, and mussels)—570 million years ago

b. 47 cm: First fish— 470 million years ago

c. 35 cm: First amphibians (early animals that were like frogs, toads, and salamanders)— 350 million years ago

d. 31 cm: First reptiles (early animals that were like dinosaurs, lizards, and snakes)—310 million years ago

e. 22.5 cm: First dinosaurs, first mammals—225 million years ago

f. 14 cm: First birds— 140 million years ago

g. 6.5 cm: Last dinosaurs— 65 million years ago

h. 2 mm: First humans— 2 million years ago

i. 0 mm: Today

THINK AND WRITE

1. Describe in words, not numbers, how long dinosaurs lived on Earth compared with the whole history of Earth. Do the same for fish.

2. RECOGNIZING TIME/SPACE RELATIONSHIPS The history of Earth is measured in time. But your time line is measured in distance. Explain how time and distance are related on your time line.

The Fossil History of the Horse

From doing the last activity, you know that it takes a very long time for animals and plants to change. Scientists use fossils they have found to trace the history of some plants and animals.

By digging up fossil bones and teeth, scientists have learned a lot about how horses have changed over time. Scientists know that horses looked much different 50 million years ago from the way they look today. The fossils of horses provide a record of how they have changed over time.

The first ancestor of the horse evolved about 50 million years ago. It was about as big as a medium-size dog. It had four toes on its feet instead of hoofs. Look at the drawing to see how the horse's hoofs evolved.

The shape of the teeth show that the earliest horses ate leaves and other soft plant parts. Slowly, the teeth changed and became flatter. These changes made the teeth better for grinding tough plants like grasses. Today's horses eat this kind of tough plant food.

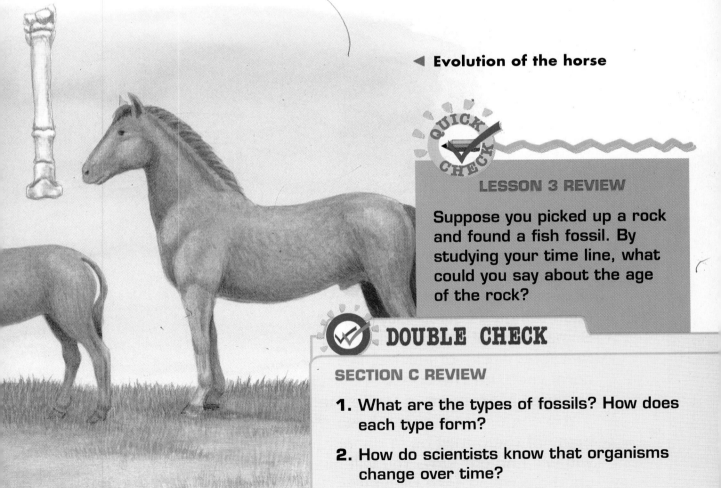

◀ **Evolution of the horse**

QUICK CHECK

LESSON 3 REVIEW

Suppose you picked up a rock and found a fish fossil. By studying your time line, what could you say about the age of the rock?

✓ DOUBLE CHECK

SECTION C REVIEW

1. What are the types of fossils? How does each type form?

2. How do scientists know that organisms change over time?

National Treasures

The land and water of our country are national treasures. The land is the source of many minerals. Minerals are needed to produce such things as electricity and steel. Some parts of the country have fantastic works of nature, like the coral reefs off the coast of Florida and Death Valley National Monument in California.

You can use and enjoy these treasures today. But many of them may be in danger. As you read on, you will find out why. You will also discover how you can help save these treasures.

1 USING RESOURCES WISELY

You switch on an electric light. A lump of coal was probably burned to generate the electricity. You throw an empty can in the garbage. There goes another bit of aluminum. Well, Earth has plenty more coal and aluminum, doesn't it? Yes, but what happens when all the coal and aluminum are used up?

Running Out of Resources

What are resources? How do we use them? Where do they come from?

Coal and aluminum are examples of natural resources. A **natural resource** is any useful material that comes from Earth. Earth has two kinds of resources.

Renewable resources can be replaced during an average human lifetime (about 75 years). Resources that come from living things, such as wood from trees, are renewable.

Either **nonrenewable resources** can't be replaced once they are used or it would take a very, very long time for them to be replaced. Oil and minerals must be used carefully because they are nonrenewable resources. Usually, soil is also considered a nonrenewable resource, since it takes a very long time to form soil that is good for growing things.

▲ Soil like this takes hundreds of years to form.

▲ Oil, a nonrenewable resource, is removed from the Earth using wells like these.

THINK ABOUT IT

Write three ways that you could use nonrenewable resources wisely.

ACTIVITY

Resources for the Future

Resources are being used up at a faster rate than ever before. How is this happening? You can find out by doing this activity.

DO THIS

1 Fill the bowls with popcorn.

2 Fourteen students should each draw an index card out of a paper bag. The cards have these labels:

2 cards — You

4 cards — Child

8 cards — Grandchild

3 Each student should take a lunch bag.

4 The students who drew the You cards should go to the bowls and fill their lunch bags with popcorn. Record the amount of popcorn taken and the amount left—for example, $\frac{1}{2}$ bowl taken, $3\frac{1}{2}$ bowls left.

MATERIALS
- popcorn
- 4 bowls
- 14 index cards
- 15 small lunch bags
- Science Log data sheet

5 Now the students with the Child cards should fill their bags with popcorn. Record the amount of popcorn taken and the amount left.

6 Finally, the students with the Grandchild cards should divide the popcorn that is left and put it in their bags. How much popcorn did each "grandchild" get?

THINK AND WRITE

1. The popcorn in this activity was a model for a resource. How would you describe the way the resource was used?

2. Suppose there is a fourth group of 16 students called Great-grandchildren. You are instructed to be sure that each "great-grandchild" gets at least $\frac{1}{2}$ bag of popcorn. What would you need to do to be sure enough popcorn is left for them?

3. CLASSIFYING/ORDERING   When you classify objects, you put them into a group of things that are like them. In this activity, what type of resource did the popcorn represent? Why did you classify the popcorn as this type of resource?

Looking Back You may have noticed that the number of people increased from You to Children to Grandchildren. This increase represents the way the world's population has been growing for at least the last 400 years.

The more people there are on Earth, the more resources that are needed to support them all. The increase in the number of people is part of the reason our natural resources are being used up. It is also an important reason for being careful with our resources.

Destroying the Land to Get Resources

Resources that come from the land have to be removed from the land. These resources may be rocks, such as coal, marble, and granite. Or the resources may be minerals within the rocks. These useful minerals are called *ores.*

In some places, the resources are hidden deep in the ground. To get at these resources, mines with deep shafts and tunnels are built. Often the tunnels are not high enough for the miners to stand up. ▶

◀ In other places, the resources are near the surface of the land. Then they're easier and less expensive to remove. But to remove them, miners must strip away the soil and rock on the surface and dig deep pits. This kind of mining is called *strip mining.* The Kennecot copper mine, shown here, is the largest strip mine in the world. Look carefully at the picture to see the cranes parked in the mine.

In strip mining, a bulldozer or other earth-moving machine is used to cut large pieces of Earth's surface into strips. These strips are removed and taken to factories where the ore is separated from the rock.

But what's left behind? A gigantic hole in the ground. All the fertile topsoil needed by plants is gone.

▶

◀ Can the land be restored or returned to its original condition? One way to do this is to save and store the topsoil. Then, after the coal, aluminum, or copper is taken from the ground, the topsoil can be put back. Young trees can be planted. In recent years, laws have been passed to make mining companies restore the land after it is mined.

This picture shows a strip mine that was restored. Now it is a lake with a park around it.

THINK ABOUT IT

How are rock and mineral resources removed from the land?

Recycle It!

There's another way to save resources and land. Don't throw away anything made of a nonrenewable resource. What should you do with an aluminum can when it's empty? Recycle it by sending it to a collecting station! Then it will be sent to a factory where it can be melted down and made into new products. How much of a nonrenewable resource can one person save? Here's a way to find out.

DO THIS

❶ Collect all the aluminum cans and other aluminum products you and your family use in a week. Rinse them out and put them in a trash bag.

MATERIALS

- aluminum used by your family in one week
- large plastic trash bag
- bathroom scale
- graph paper
- Science Log data sheet

❷ Weigh the bag of aluminum and record the weight. You can do this by first weighing just yourself and then weighing yourself while you're holding the bag. Subtract your weight from the weight of you and the bag together. That will give you the weight of the bag.

❸ Share your data with your classmates. Record the weights of their bags, too.

❹ Make a bar graph showing all the weights. You can use the graph below as a model.

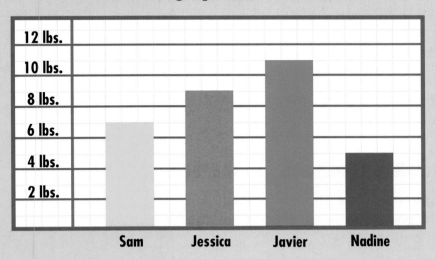

12 lbs.				
10 lbs.				
8 lbs.				
6 lbs.				
4 lbs.				
2 lbs.				
	Sam	Jessica	Javier	Nadine

THINK AND WRITE

1. What was the greatest weight of aluminum collected? What was the least weight collected?

2. What was the total weight collected by the class?

3. What might explain the difference between the greatest and least weights collected?

4. Suppose that for every week in the year, you collect the same amount of aluminum as you did in this activity. How much would you recycle in a year? If the whole class recycles, how much aluminum would be recycled in a year?

LESSON 1 REVIEW

Think about the resources you use each week. Make a list of them. Divide the list into renewable and nonrenewable resources. How can you reduce the uses of each resource?

2 SAVING OUR NATIONAL PARKS

As the population of the United States has grown, more and more land has been needed for farms and factories. To protect the natural beauty of our country, a national park system was created. But now many parks are in danger because of the huge numbers of people that visit them. What kinds of dangers do the national parks face? In this lesson, you will find out.

Tour Our National Parks

There are 50 national parks in the United States. These are places where people go to see some of the natural wonders of our country.

▲ Hawai'i Volcanoes National Park is famous for its fiery mountains.

◄ Redwood National Park in California has the tallest trees on Earth.

◄ Yellowstone National Park covers parts of Wyoming, Idaho, and Montana. Many people come to see its geysers. Geysers are springs that send up fountains of hot water from inside the Earth. Yellowstone has more geysers than any other place in the world.

Visitors can walk beside an underground river in Mammoth Cave, Kentucky. Inside the cave, they can also see columns made of stone hanging from rocky ceilings or rising from rocky floors. ►

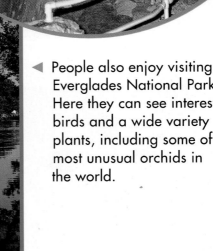

◄ People also enjoy visiting Everglades National Park. Here they can see interesting birds and a wide variety of plants, including some of the most unusual orchids in the world.

Millions of people every year come to national parks in cars, vans, campers, buses, and, in some cases, boats. That is where the problem begins.

Hikers come to see the unspoiled beauty of a national park. But they often trample trailside flowers and plants. Some thoughtless visitors litter the woods with garbage. ▶

Some people like to let others know that they've been somewhere. So they may be tempted to carve their names on a tree or spray paint them on a rock or building. But carving may injure or kill the tree. And paint is ugly compared with mountain flowers or a sparkling granite boulder. The natural beauty is no longer natural and untouched. ▶

The people who visit national parks need places to sleep, to eat, and to shop. Their gas tanks must be filled. Some areas in national parks look more like shopping centers than parks. As these areas grow, they take over the living space of plants and animals. The natural area shrinks. ▼

Park rangers try to make sure that people obey park rules. But the number of people visiting parks is increasing faster than the number of rangers. So other ways have to be found to protect national parks. ▼

Here are some suggestions that have been made to protect national parks. Read them carefully before you do the activity that follows.

- Limit the number of people who can visit a national park at any one time.
- Make people park their cars outside the park. Have buses or other large vehicles move people into and around the park. This would reduce traffic and air pollution.
- Reduce the number of restaurants, snack bars, shops, and gas stations in the park.
- Limit activities that harm living things in the park, such as hiking away from the trails.
- Provide more money to study how to preserve national parks.
- Provide money to educate people about the value of national parks and the ways to keep them healthy.

▲ Park shuttle buses, such as these in Glacier National Park in Montana, reduce the number of vehicles in the parks.

THINK ABOUT IT

How do people harm our national parks?

ACTIVITY

How Can We Save Our National Parks?

MATERIALS

- yarn
- 7 index cards
- tape recorder or video camera
- Science Log data sheet

Different people have different answers for this question. For example, a souvenir-shop owner might have a very different opinion than a park ranger has. In this activity, you and your classmates will investigate the opinions of different people. Then you will decide what you think should be done to save our national parks.

DO THIS

1 Work with six other students. The members of your group should play the roles of the following people:

10-year-old park visitor

adult park visitor

park ranger

souvenir-shop owner

scientist who studies park plants

local member of Congress

reporter

② Make a name tag for each member of the group. Make them like the ones shown in the picture.

③ Your group will discuss the suggestions listed on page D87 from the points of view of the people you are playing. Which of the suggestions do you recommend? Which are you against? Why?

④ Use a tape recorder or video camera to record the discussion. Then review the tape and make notes about each person's ideas.

THINK AND WRITE

Based on the discussion, suggest one or more ways to save our national parks that would be acceptable to all the people in the group. This might require some or all of the people to give up something they want.

LESSON 2 REVIEW

① What is the main reason many national parks are in danger?

② "Leave only footprints. Take only memories." This is a rule for visiting parks. Explain what it means.

 DOUBLE CHECK

SECTION D REVIEW

1. What is the difference between a renewable resource and a nonrenewable resource? Give examples.

2. When might a renewable resource become nonrenewable?

3. How might the discovery of copper in a national park affect the park?

I REFLECT

It's time to think about the ideas you have discovered during your investigations. Think, too, about your many accomplishments.

SUMMARIZE

Answer the following in your Science Log.

1. What **I Wonder** questions have you answered in your investigations? What new questions have you asked?

2. What have you discovered about rocks, minerals, Earth's history, and Earth's resources? How have your ideas changed?

3. Did any of your discoveries surprise you? Explain.

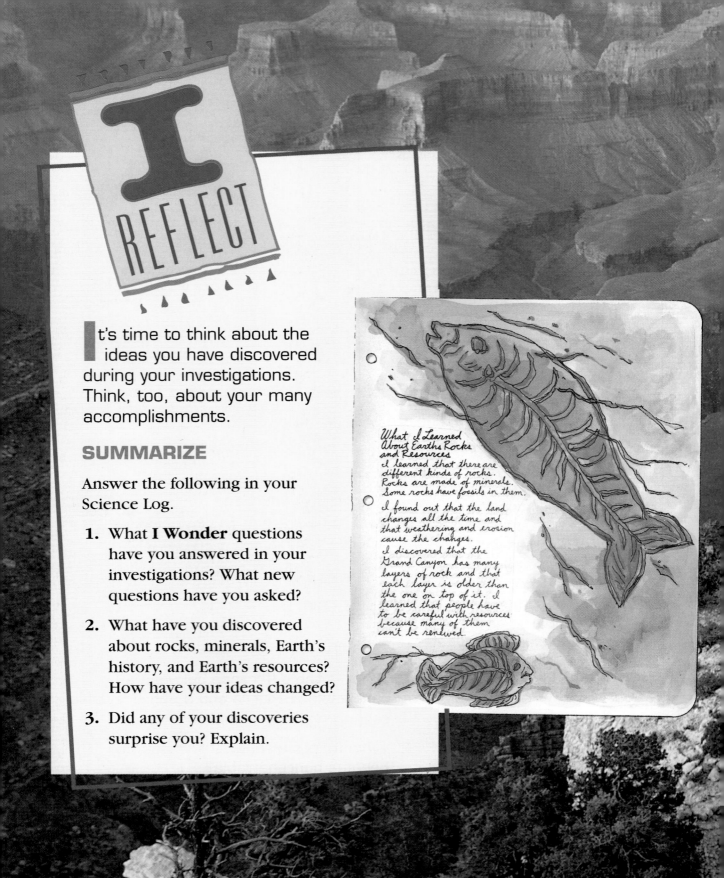

What I Learned About Earths Rocks and Resources

I learned that there are different kinds of rocks. Rocks are made of minerals. Some rocks have fossils in them.

I found out that the land changes all the time and that weathering and erosion cause the changes.

I discovered that the Grand Canyon has many layers of rock and that each layer is older than the one on top of it. I learned that people have to be careful with resources because many of them can't be renewed.

CONNECT IDEAS

1. Explain how a sedimentary rock can become a metamorphic rock.

2. How did the Grand Canyon form?

3. How is a cast fossil different from a mold fossil?

4. How have scientists determined that plants and animals have changed over time?

5. What are natural resources, and how do we use them?

SCIENCE PORTFOLIO

❶ Complete your Science Experiences Record.

❷ Choose one or two samples of your best work from each section to include in your Science Portfolio.

❸ On A Guide to My Science Portfolio, tell why you chose each sample.

SHARE

Scientists share their discoveries and ideas and learn from one another. How can you share what you've learned?

Decide

▶ what you want to say.

▶ what the best way is to get your message across.

Share

▶ what you did and why.

▶ what worked and what didn't work.

▶ what conclusions you have drawn.

▶ what else you'd like to find out.

Find Out

▶ what classmates liked about what you shared—and why.

▶ what questions your classmates have.

Science is more than discoveries —it is also what you do with those discoveries. How might you use what you have learned about the land?

► Tell people why it's important not to throw away metal products like those made of aluminum and copper.

► Collect rocks and set up a rock collection to show other students about the rocks in your area.

► Make a poster showing the fossils that can be found in your area. Use the poster to teach your family and friends about fossils.

► Set up a recycling program in your community or school.

► Join a group that is helping preserve national, state, or local parks.

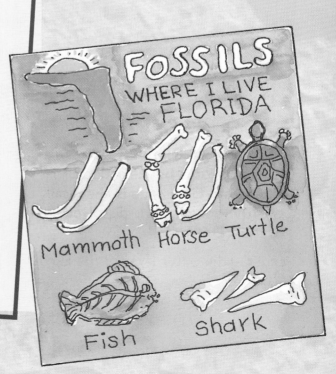

THE LANGUAGE OF SCIENCE

The language of science helps people communicate clearly when they talk about nature. Here are some vocabulary words you can use when you talk about rocks, the land, and the history of the Earth with friends, family, and others.

erosion—the carrying away of weathered material by water, wind, or glaciers. Erosion of the Grand Canyon was caused, in part, by the Colorado River. **(D49)**

fossil—the preserved trace or remains of a once-living thing. Examples are an imprint, a mold, and a cast. Fossils are also found in glacial ice, amber, and tar pits. **(D59)**

igneous rock—rock that forms from red-hot liquid rock. Volcanoes produce igneous rocks. **(D13)**

Obsidian is an igneous rock. ▶

chemical weathering—the breaking down of rocks by the action of chemicals. Limestone is chemically weathered when it is dissolved by water. **(D44)**

crust—the outer layer of the Earth. **(D31)**

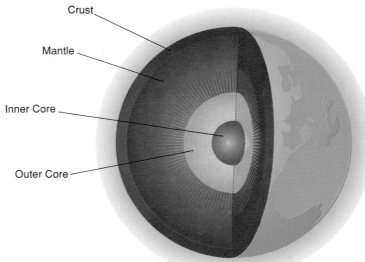

Crust

Mantle

Inner Core

Outer Core

landforms—features of Earth's crust, such as mountains, valleys, and plains. **(D32)**

metamorphic rock—rock that forms from rocks when they are heated and squeezed in the Earth. **(D15)**

minerals—the materials that make up rocks. **(D20)**

natural resource—any useful material that comes from the Earth. **(D77)**

nonrenewable resource—either a resource that cannot be replaced once it is used up or a resource that would take a very, very long time to be replaced. The formation of new coal, for example, would take millions of years. **(D77)**

physical weathering—the breaking apart of rocks by wind, water, ice, and plants. The roots of plants can grow in the cracks in rocks and break the rocks apart. **(D41)**

▲ Roots of plants can cause weathering.

renewable resource—a resource that can be replaced in a reasonable amount of time. Wood is a renewable resource because new trees can grow to replace those cut down. **(D77)**

▲ Wood is a renewable resource.

sea level—the average level of the sea where it meets the land. **(D35)**

sedimentary rock—rock that forms from sediments that harden under conditions of extreme heat and pressure. Limestone is a sedimentary rock. **(D14)**

weathering—the breaking down of rocks by water, plants, ice, wind, and chemicals. **(D40)**

REFERENCE HANDBOOK

Safety in the Classroom

Doing activities in science can be fun, but you need to be sure you do them safely. It is up to you, your teacher, and your classmates to make your classroom a safe place for science activities.

Think about what causes most accidents in everyday life—being careless, not paying attention, and showing off. The same kinds of behavior cause accidents in the science classroom.

Here are some ways to make your classroom a safe place.

THINK AHEAD.

Study the steps of the activity so you know what to expect. If you have any questions about the steps, ask your teacher to explain. Be sure you understand any safety symbols that are shown in the activity.

WATCH YOUR EYES.

Wear safety goggles anytime you are directed to do so. If you should ever get any substance in your eyes, tell your teacher right away.

BE NEAT.

Keep your work area clean. If you have long hair, pull it back so it doesn't get in the way. If you have long sleeves, roll them or push them up to keep them away from your experiment.

OOPS!

If you should have an accident that causes a spill or breaks something, or if you get cut, tell your teacher right away.

YUCK!

Never eat or drink anything during a science activity unless you are told to do so by your teacher.

KEEP IT CLEAN.

Always clean up when you have finished your activity. Put everything away and wipe your work area. Last of all, wash your hands.

DON'T GET SHOCKED.

Sometimes you need to use electric appliances, such as lamps, in an activity. You always need to be careful around electricity. Be sure that electric cords are in a safe place where you can't trip over them. Don't ever pull a plug out of an outlet by pulling on the cord.

Measuring Liquids

Use a beaker, a measuring cup, or a graduated cylinder to measure liquids accurately.

Containers for measuring liquids are made of clear or translucent materials so that you can see the liquid inside them. On the outside of each of these measuring tools, you will see lines and numbers that make up a scale. On most of the containers used by scientists, the scale is in milliliters (mL).

DO THIS

1 Pour the liquid you want to measure into one of the measuring containers. Make sure your measuring container is on a flat, stable surface, with the measuring scale facing you.

2 Look at the liquid through the container. Move so that your eyes are even with the surface of the liquid in the container.

3 To read the volume of the liquid, find the scale line that is even with the top of the liquid. In narrow containers, the surface of the liquid may look curved. Take your reading at the lowest point of the curve.

▲ There are 32 mL of liquid in this graduated cylinder.

4 Sometimes the surface of the liquid may not be exactly even with a line. In that case, you will need to estimate the volume of the liquid. Decide which line the liquid is closer to, and use that number.

▲ There are 27 mL of liquid in this beaker.

Using a Thermometer

Determine temperature readings of the air and most liquids by using a thermometer with a standard scale.

Most thermometers are thin tubes of glass that are filled with a red or silver liquid. As the temperature goes up, the liquid in the tube rises. As the temperature goes down, the liquid sinks. The tube is marked with lines and numbers that provide a temperature scale in degrees. Scientists use the Celsius scale to measure temperature. A temperature reading of 27 degrees Celsius is written 27°C.

DO THIS

❶ Place the thermometer in the liquid whose temperature you want to record, but don't rest the bulb of the thermometer on the bottom or side of the container. If you are measuring the temperature of the air, make sure that the thermometer is not in direct sunlight or in line with a direct light source.

❷ Move so that your eyes are even with the liquid in the thermometer.

❸ If you are measuring a material that is not being heated or cooled, wait about two minutes for the reading to become stable. Find the scale line that meets the top of the liquid in the thermometer, and read the temperature.

❹ If the material you are measuring is being heated or cooled, you will not be able to wait before taking your measurements. Measure as quickly as you can.

The temperature of this liquid is 27°C. ▶

Making a Thermometer

If you don't have a thermometer, you can make a
simple one easily. The simple thermometer won't
give you an exact temperature reading, but you
can use it to tell if the temperature is going up
or going down.

DO THIS

1 Add colored water to the jar until it is
nearly full.

2 Place the straw in the jar. Finish filling
the jar with water, but leave about 1 cm
of space at the top.

3 Lift the straw until 10 cm of it sticks up out of the jar. Use
the clay to seal the mouth of the jar.

4 Use the dropper to add colored water to the straw until
the straw is at least half full.

5 On the straw, mark the level of the water. "S" stands
for *start.*

6 To get an idea of how your thermometer works, place
the jar in a bowl of ice. Wait several minutes, and then
mark the new water level on the straw. This new water
level should be marked C for *cold.*

7 Take the jar out of the bowl of ice, and let it return to
room temperature. Next, place the jar in a bowl of
warm water. Wait several minutes, and then mark the
new water level on the straw. This level can be labeled
W for *warm.*

W
S
C

▶ You can use a thermometer like
this to decide if the temperature
of a liquid or the air is going up
or down.

Using a Balance

Use a balance to measure an object's mass. Mass is the amount of matter an object has.

Most balances look like the one shown. They have two pans. In one pan, you place the object you want to measure. In the other pan, you place standard masses. Standard masses are objects that have a known mass. Grams are the units used to measure mass for most scientific activities.

DO THIS

❶ First, make certain the empty pans are balanced. They are in balance if the pointer is at the middle mark on the base. If the pointer is not at this mark, move the slider to the right or left. Your teacher will help if you cannot balance the pans.

◀ These pans are balanced and ready to be used to find the mass of an object.

❷ Place the object you wish to measure in one pan. The pointer will move toward the pan without the object in it.

❸ Add the standard masses to the other pan. As you add masses, you should see the pointer begin to move. When the pointer is at the middle mark again, the pans are balanced.

❹ Add the numbers on the masses you used. The total is the mass of the object you measured.

These pans are unbalanced. ▶

Margie, Anna, and Kevin designed a way to test their hypothesis. They also planned a way to collect the information. Another word for information is *data.* The next important step in their investigation was to find a way to *record the data.*

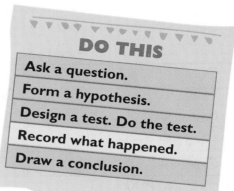

DO THIS

Ask a question.

Form a hypothesis.

Design a test. Do the test.

Record what happened.

Draw a conclusion.

Kevin, Margie, and Anna sat at a table with what seemed like hundreds of soup-can labels in front of them.

"Oh, no," Anna said. "What are we going to do? How can we make any sense out of all of this?"

Margie frowned. "It's really a mess. But what if we started by just separating the labels into groups? Then we could make a chart. We could label one column *Creamy Soups* and one *Watery Soups* and list the grams of fat in a serving of each kind of soup. Most of the labels list an eight-ounce serving, so we could use those and throw the rest away."

Kevin said, "Good idea. We could list each kind of soup and the number of grams of fat it has in the right column."

"Oh, I see," Anna said. "Then we can add up the total grams of fat in the soups when we get done with our test."

Margie agreed. But then she thought about something else. "There's one more thing we have to remember. We must have exactly the same number of creamy soups and watery soups. If we don't, it would not be a fair test."

Kevin, Anna, and Margie sorted their labels. You can see part of their data in this chart.

Data from Soup Labels		
Names of Soups	Fat in Creamy Soups/ Per 8 Ounces	Fat in Watery Soups/ Per 8 Ounces
Cream of Potato	3g	
Cream of Broccoli	5g	
Cream of Mushroom	7g	
Chicken Noodle		3g
Bean with Bacon		4g
Beef Noodle		4g

"But this chart is hard to read," Margie said.

"I know," Anna said. "Let's make a bar graph. We can have two bars to show the grams of fat in watery and creamy soups."

Kevin drew the bar graph you see here.

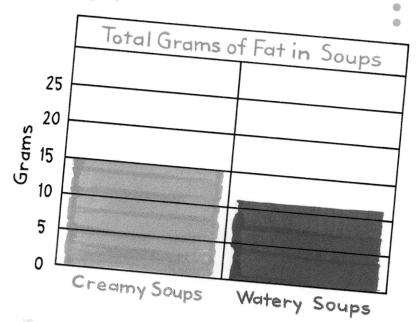

After you have collected the data, you need to see what it tells you about whether your answer to the question was correct or incorrect. You do this by seeing if the data supports your hypothesis and by *drawing a conclusion*.

DO THIS

| Ask a question. |
| Form a hypothesis. |
| Design a test. Do the test. |
| Record what happened. |
| Draw a conclusion. |

"Well," Anna said, "what do you think?"

"I don't know," Kevin said. "It seems to me that creamy soups and watery soups can have the same amount of fat."

"That's what it looks like to me," Margie said. "Look here," she said as she pointed to the bar graph. "These are nearly equal."

"They are," Anna said. "Are you surprised? I am."

"I am, too," Margie said. "Water doesn't have any fat, but some watery soups sure do."

"I think we've found out something important that we can share with the class," Kevin said. "Maybe a lot of people think the way we did!"

"You're right," Anna said. "Let's make a poster to show everyone what we found out."

If your first answer is not correct, you have not failed. Margie, Anna, and Kevin learned something surprising about soups. The data they collected didn't support their hypothesis that watery soups would have less fat than creamy soups. This often occurs with an investigation. When something happens that you don't expect, you can learn from it. You can use that information to start asking other questions. You may need to form a different hypothesis and design a new experiment. However, you are able to build on what you know.

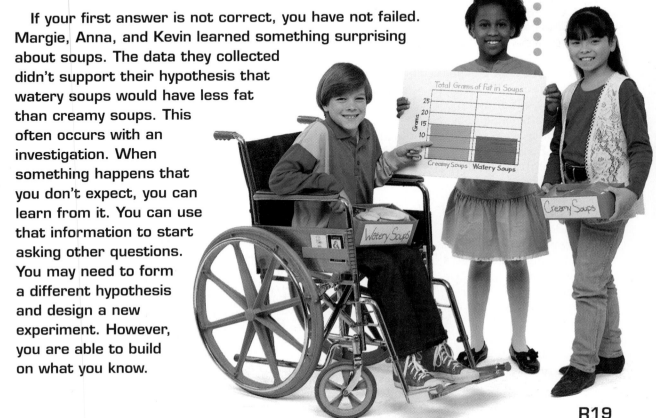

INDEX

Note: Page numbers in italics indicate illustrations.

J

K

L

Morgan/Rainbow; C87, Peter Menzel; C87, Peter Menzel; C88, Peter Menzel; C89, Peter Menzel;C90-C91, (bg), Alan Kearney/FPG; C91(l), Roy Morsch/Stock Market, The; C91 (r), Dan McCoy/Rainbow; C92-C93 (bg), Phillip M. Prosen/The Image Bank; C94(t), Montes De Oca/FPG International; C94(b), Fundamental Photographs; C95(l), E. R. Degginger/Color-Pic; C95 (r), Westlight; C96, Joe Baraban/The Stock Market.

Unit D: Harcourt Brace & Company Photographs: D4-D5, D6(t), D7(b), D8, D9, D10-D11, D19, D21, D24, D25(b), D31, D34, D43, D45 (all), D50, D53(l), D60, D61, D72, D73, D79, D82(l), D88, D92(t), D92(b), D93.

All Other Photographs: Unit D Divider: John Kieffer/Peter Arnold; D1, Tom Till; D2-D3(bg), Tom Till; D3(inset), Tom Till; D7(t), Gamma Liaison; D12(bg) Comstock; D12(t), Robert Falls/Bruce Coleman, Inc.; D12(b), E. R. Degginger/Color-Pic; D13t), Stephen Frisch/Stock, Boston; D13(b), Kevin Syms/David R. Frazier; D14(t), Tom Till; D14(b), William E. Ferguson; D15(l), E. R. Degginger/Color-Pic; D15(r), E. R. Degginger/Color-Pic; D18, Ferdinando Scianna/Magnum; D20(l), E. R. Degginger/Color-Pic; D20(r), E. R. Degginger/Color-Pic; D22(l), William E. Ferguson; D22(r), David R. Frazier; D23(tr), David. R. Frazier; D23 (bl), E. R. Degginger/Color-Pic; D23(bc), Art Resource; D23(br), E. R. Degginger/Color-Pic; D23(cr), E. R. Degginger/Color-Pic; D23 , Ron Kimball; D23, (tl), William E. Ferguson; D25(t), Eric A. Wessman/Stock, Boston; D26-D27(bg) Tom Till; D26(t), Tom Till; D26 (b), Tom Till; D27, Tom Till; D28 (t), Museum Of New Mexico; D28 (b), San Ildefonso polychrome, ca. 1922. Courtesy The Southwest Museum, Los Angeles ; D29 (t), Laboratory of Anthropology, Santa Fe.; D29(c), Laboratory of Anthropology, Santa Fe.; D29(b), Laboratory of Anthropology, Santa Fe.; D30 (bg) William E. Ferguson; D30 (t), John Kieffer/Peter Arnold, Inc.; D30(b), Tom Till; D32Ed Cooper Photography; D33t), Jim Steinberg/Photo Researchers; D33(b), The Image Works; D40, Nathen Benn/Stock, Boston; D40 (t), BPS/Terraphotographics; D41, (b)BPS/Terraphotographics; D42-D43(bg) Runk/Schoenberger/Grant Heilman; D44, BPS/Terraphotographics; D45b), Tom Till; D46(t), Tom Till; D46(c), Tom Till; D46(b), Joe Carrillo/Stock, Boston; D47 (t), Tom Till; D47(b), Tom Till; D48, Tom Till; D49(tr), Henry K. Kaiser/Leo de Wys Inc.; D49(bl), BPS/Terraphotographics; D49 (br), Dan Suzio/Photo Researchers; D49 (cl), Tom Till; D51 (l), Spencer Swanger/Tom Stack & Assoc.; D51 (r), Jack Fields/Photo Researchers; D51b), Ed Cooper Photography; D52(t), Greg Ryan & Sally Beyer; D52(b), Randall Hyman/Stock, Boston; D53 (r), David Wells/The Image Works; D54, Steve McCutcheon; D56(bg), William E. Ferguson; D56 (t), Bob Daemmrich/Stock, Boston; D56(inset) Tom Till; D58 (b), Peter Arnold/Peter Arnold, Inc.; D59 (t), Ken Lucas/BPS/Terraphotographics; D59(b), William E. Ferguson; D59 (c), J&L Weber/Peter Arnold, Inc.; D62 (t), William E. Ferguson; D62(b), Sinclair Stammers/Photo Researchers; D62, William E. Ferguson; D63 (t), B. Miller/BPS/Terraphotographics; D63(b), William E. Ferguson; D64(t), Francois Gohier/Photo Researchers; D64 (b), Tom McHugh/Nat. Museum of Nat. History; D65, William E. Ferguson; D66 (t), Saunders/BPS/Terraphotographics; D66(c), Itar-Tass/Sovoto; D67(b), Photo Researchers; D67(bg), William E. Ferguson; D70(l) William E. Ferguson; D70(r), William E. Ferguson; D71(l), Tom McHugh/National Museum of Natural History; D71((c), J&L Weber/Peter Arnold, Inc.; D71(r), PHoto Researchers; D76, (bg), Art Wolfe/AllStock; D76 (t), Stephen Frink/Waterhouse Stock Photo; D76(t), Terry Donnelly/Dembinsky Photo Assoc.; D76 (b), Gordon Wiltsie/Peter Arnold, Inc.; D77(b), Crandall/The Image Works; D78-D79 (bg), Art Wolfe/AllStock; D80(l), Tom Myers; D80 (r), Bill Gallery/Stock, Boston; D81 (t), Billy Barnes; D81(b), Cary Wolinsky/Stock, Boston; D82(r), Martin Miller/Positive Image; D84(l), Ed Cooper Photography; D84 (r), Joseph Solem/Camera Hawaii; D85(t), J. Robert Stottlemyer/Biological Photo Service; D85 (c), W.L. McCoy/McCoy's Image Studio; D85(b), Bob & Ira Spring; D86(t), Julie Houck/Stock, Boston; D86(c), Jeff Foott/Tom Stack & Assoc.; D86(c), David Young-Wolf/PhotoEdit; D87, (l), Laurance B. Aiuppy; D87(r), Laurance B.Aiuppy; D90-D91(bg), Ruch Buzzelli/Tom Stack & Assoc.; D91 (l), Ken Lucas/Biological Photo Service; D91(r), Dembinski Photo Assoc.; D94, (inset) Breck P. Kent/Earth Scenes; D94, Franco Salmoiraghi/The Stock Market; D95, Art Wolfe/AllStock.

Unit E: Harcourt Brace & Company Photographs: E7, E8, E9, E10-E11, E14, E22, E23, E25, E26, E36, E39, E40, E44, E53, E57(tl), E61, E62, E65(b), E76 (t).

All Other Photographs: Unit E Divider: H. Mark Weidman; E1, Tom Till; E2-E3(bg), Tom Till; E3, (inset) Thomas R. Fletcher/Stock, Boston; E6, Murial Orans; E12(t), J. Lotter/Tom Stack & Assoc.; E12(inset) E. R. Degginger/Color-Pic; E12(border) FPG Internatinal; E13, H. Mark Weidman; E15(r), Coco McCoy/Rainbow; E15(r), Ira Spring; E18(t), Tom Stack & Assoc.; E18(b), John Gerlach/Tom Stack & Assoc.; E21 (t), H. Mark Weidman; E21 (c), William E. Ferguson; E21(b), Murial Orans; E21(bg), Brain Parker/Tom Stacks & Assoc.; E30, H. Mark Weidman; E38, (bg), Superstock; E38, (t), Ed Cooper PhotoraphE; E38, (inset) William E. Ferguson; E41 (l), Mark C. Burnett; E41 (r), Mark C. Burnett; E41 (b), Mark C. Burnett; E42, Charlie Ott Photography/Photo Reseachers; E43(c), William E. Ferguson Photography; E43(b), BPS/Terraphotographics; E47 (t), Rod Plank/Dembinsky Photo Association; E48, Stephen E. Cornelius/Photo Researchers; E50(bg), Uniphoto; E50(t), Uniphoto; E50, (inset) Aaron Haupt/David R. Frazier; E51, (t), Erich Geduldig/Naturbild/OKAPIA/Photo Researchers, Inc.; E51(b), David E. Frazier; E54 (c), E. R. Degginger/Color-Pic; E54(tl), E. R. Degginger/Color-Pic; E54(tr), Jerome Wexler/Photo Researchers; E54(bl), Phil Degginger/Color-Pic; E54(br), E. R. Degginger/Color-Pic; E55 (tl), Hermann Eisenbeiss/Photo Researchers; E55(tr), Michael P. Gadomski/Photo Researchers; E55 (bl), Murial Orans; E55(br), William E. Ferguson; E56(tl), Alvin E. Staffan/Photo Researchers; E56 (tr), E. R. Degginger/Color-Pic; E56 (bl), Aaron Haupt/David E. Frazier; E56 (br), M.L.Dembinsky, Jr. / Dembinsky Photo Assoc.; E56(cl), Kenneth Murray/Photo Researchers; E56(cr), William E. Ferguson; E57(tr), E. R. Degginger/Color-Pic; E57(bl), Gary Retherford/Photo Researchers; E57(br), Kjell B. Sandved/Photo Researchers; E59(l), Dale Nichols/Rich Franco Photography; E59(r), Terry Donnelly/Dembinsky Photo Assos.; E64-E65(t), G.V. Faint/The Image Bank; E66 (t), E. R. Degginger/Color-Pic; E66(b), Harry Rogers/Photo Researchers; E67(t), Bonnie Rauch/Photo Researchers; E67(c), David R. Frazier; E67(b), Leonide Principe/Photo Researchers; E68(t), E. R. Degginger/Color-Pic; E68 (c), E. R. Degginger/Color-Pic; E68 (b), Camera Hawaii; E69 (t), William E.Ferguson; E69 (c), Dwight Kuhn; E69(b), E. R. Degginger/Color-Pic; E70, Walter Chandoha,; E71(c), Ian J. Adams/ Dembinsky Photo Assoc.; E71 (c), William E. Ferguson; E71(tr), Willard Clay/Dembinsky Photo Assoc.; E71 (bl), Ken Brate/Photo Researchers Inc.,E71 (br), Scott Camazine/Photo Researchers Inc.,E72 (t), Ronald Nagata, Sr.; E72-E73(b), Ronald Nagata, Sr.; E74(inset) David R. Frazier; E74-75(bg), William M. Partington/Photo Researchers Inc.; E75(inset) Gary Braasch/Woodfin Camp & Assoc.; E76 (t),Tony Freeman/PhotoEdit; E77(t), Larry Lefever/Grant Heilman ; E77 (b), Hank Morgan/Photo Researchers Inc.; E78(l), Runk Schoenberger/Grant Heilman .